Blackshirts and Roses

An Autobiography
by
John Charnley

Black House Publishing Ltd
London

Blackshirts and Roses

An Autobiography

by

John Charnley

1st Published 1990 by Brockingday Publications
This Edition Published 2012

ISBN-13: 978-1-908476-43-2

Black House Publishing Ltd
Kemp House
152 City Road
London
UNITED KINGDOM
EC1V 2NX

www.blackhousepublishing.co.uk
Email: info@blackhousepublishing.co.uk

"To strive, to seek, to find, and not to yield"
Ulysses: Tennyson

To my wife
"Mea Maxima Gracias"

Contents

Foreword

IN the last year of his life, John Charnley wrote to his MP Ronald Fearn, requesting his assistance in "clearing my name of any suggestion of potential traitorous behaviour."

In a letter to Mr Fearn, dated April 1988, John explained that after applying to the Public Records Office at Kew with reference to his detention and tribunal hearings, he was informed that his own records had been destroyed.

"What chance then, do I have? I am now nearing the end of my days and time for me is short. I am a chair-bound invalid, but would make the effort to see you if this is your wish. I have nothing to hide and am proud of my behaviour. I remain true to my beliefs."

Mr Fearn referred John Charnley's case to the Home Office Minister John Patten. In a reply to Mr Fearn dated May 17, Mr Patten confirmed that the papers relating to John's detention "were not among those retained for permanent preservation at the Public Records Office.

"I appreciate Mr Charnley's continuing concern over his detention, but in the absence of these papers there are no other relevant Home Office records which would be of assistance and I fear I am unable to take this matter any further."

John Charnley continued in correspondence with Ronald Fearn however. Two matters in particular exercised his concern. The first was the Bill passed by the United States Senate, compensating the 120,000 Japanese-Americans detained from 1942 until the end of the Pacific War. The cost of this legislation has been estimated at 1.35 billion dollars, and details of this handsome expression of retrospective justice were sent to the Home Secretary Douglas Hurd by the late Dr. Peter Peel, a life-long Mosley supporter, who served in the Royal Air Force from 1939 to 1946, and was a resident of the United States for 30 years until his sudden death in 1988.

"If our American ally can authorise such compensation, does this not in itself suggest that similar action should be sanctioned by our present Parliament?" asked John Charnley in a letter to Ronald Fearn in June 1988.

In the same letter, John developed a second line of attack. "A further study of the Petition of Rights which Charles I signed in 1628 — a breach of which contributed to his condemnation and execution — further encourages me to believe that you could use this advantageously.

"It clearly states that no subject of the King could be imprisoned without just cause shown. I suggest you use this ancient Parliamentary practice and apply for a Bill of Attainder against the Home Secretary, in that the phrase under which I was detained stated that the Home Secretary had 'reasonable cause to believe' that I constituted a security risk. This surely places an onus upon the Home Secretary to substantiate that 'reasonable cause to believe' subsequently produces that 'just cause has been shown'.

"Over 800 Mosley supporters were detained, and in not one instance was 'reasonable cause to believe' converted into 'just cause being shown'."

Mr. Fearn forwarded these observations to Mr. Patten at the Home Office. In his reply to the Southport MP, dated August 22, the Minister commented: "In your latest letter you ask whether the 'Petition of Human Rights 1628' could be the key to 'pardoning' persons who, like Mr. Charnley, were detained. (I am not sure whether the terms of your letter mean that you have an interest in cases other than Mr. Charnley's. I hope you will understand that I confine myself to Mr. Charnley's representations).

"Prior to the repeal in 1628 of the relevant provisions, the Petition of Right of 1627 provided that no free man may be imprisoned other than by the lawful judgement of his peers or by the law of the land. It appears that Mr. Charnley was detained under Regulation 18b of the Defence (General) Regulations 1939. That was 'the law of the land.' I can only suggest therefore, that Mr. Charnley's detention was not inconsistent with the terms of the Petition.

"In the absence of any papers, and relying on Mr. Charnley's account. ...it would seem that whilst (sic) Mr. Charnley was detained under the law as it then stood, but not convicted of any offence there is, therefore, no offence which can be pardoned. There is no power by which the Home Secretary can affect or, as it were, 'wipe out' the fact that he was detained under the exceptional powers of detention in the Defence Regulations.

I am afraid I can only confirm that there is no action which the Home Secretary could now properly take."

Chapter One

Orphanage Boy and Master Baker

A Saturday night in late September towards the end of July that warm Summer of 1933, single and 23, I was off to meet my friends for a carefree night's dancing at Southport's Floral Hall.

Hurrying down Chapel Street I was accosted outside Woolworths by a well-built man wearing a black shirt. He pushed a newspaper under my nose and said, "Buy 'The Blackshirt', Sir, one penny." It was Tommy Moran. I bought it, he never called me "Sir" again, and my life was changed forever.

I write this on my seventy-eighth birthday, an appropriate time to look back on a life that has had more than its share of ups and downs. This is my story from a Leeds orphanage via a bed-sitter in Southampton, to addressing political meetings all over the country, to internment in wartime prison camps in England and the Isle of Man; and much later, after many years of public service, to a Royal Garden Party at Buckingham Palace.

From 1933 on, one thing has remained constant, however, and in this I take some pride: my loyalty to Oswald Mosley. I had been brought up in a home where politics and economics — in those days called 'Political Economy' — were general topics of conversation. In his time, my father had walked and talked with the Socialist giants of his day: Philip Snowden, James Maxton, Jimmy Thomas and J.R. Clynes, the Lancashire lad who, from the most humble beginnings, rose to become Lord Privy Seal and Home Secretary.

In later years I was to come into contact with leading politicians such as Jennie Lee, Harold Wilson and Sydney Silverman on the Left and Ernest Marples, Enoch Powell and Michael Heseltine on the Right.

This early background sowed the seeds of my future interest in politics, but, it was two apparently insignificant incidents in Southampton that set me on the path I have followed faithfully ever since. On a Sunday morning in June 1930 I read in the Sunday Express, borrowed from my landlady, of the Resignation Speech of a Minister who had found it impossible to get the Labour Government to do anything to help the unemployed. Since I was out of work, and my dole money had just been cut from 17 shillings to 15 shillings a week, Oswald Mosley's resignation was of direct interest to me.

The other incident occurred some months later after I had found a part-time job in a baker's shop. A poorly dressed lad entered and asked for a loaf of bread, in payment for which he offered me two empty milk bottles and a penny stamp. (In those days there was a penny deposit on a milk bottle and a large loaf cost 3½ pence). It was all he had to purchase a loaf. This experience left a deep and unforgettable impression. It made me ponder deeply on what was wrong with our society.

Over the years many friends have tried to persuade me to write those memories. The first was Mosley himself. I was talking to him shortly after the publication of his autobiography "My Life" in 1968 when he suggested that my recounting of the political events of the Thirties would be a useful complement to his own. But having always been a devotee of the spoken rather than the written word, I always resisted. Now my speaking days are over, and the written word is the only means of expression left open to me. So I start my story.

I was born in Leeds on Friday in December, 1909, the youngest of six, Friday the thirteenth child. Once described by a contemporary writer on Fascism in Britain as coming from the lower middle class, I contend that I belong to no specific class. Although born in Yorkshire my forebears are from Westmorland, (now Cumbria). My father was born in Rochdale but finally settled in Blackburn. He was a bespoke tailor, and his father a textile engineer employed in a cotton mill as a maintenance operator.

His father, in turn, was a farm labourer near Keswick, the son of a smallholder, whose forebears were respectively an inn keeper, a gentleman householder, and a small farmer in Westmorland. The earliest trace that I have is dated 1787, so I suppose I can claim to come from country yeoman stock.

When I was a little under two, my mother died, leaving my father with our large family to bring up. In those days circumstances were very different to what they are today, and with no social security, my father was forced to place some of the younger children in an orphanage.

After some discussion with my maternal grandmother, a member of the Society of Friends, it was arranged that we would be sent from Blackburn, where the family was then living, to a Quaker orphanage in Cliff Lane, Hyde Park, Leeds.

One of my earliest recollections was attending Quarry Mount Council School. This was during the First World War, and during classes one of our teachers, a Miss Mitchell, never missed an opportunity of saying that she was inclined towards sympathies with Germany. In her opinion the war should not have taken place and was very unjust. It was not until many years later that I realised her comments might have made a firm impression on me, and perhaps encouraged me to question the wisdom and validity of future wars undertaken in the name of our people.

I was on holiday at Bridlington with other children from the orphanage at the outbreak of the First War, and can distinctly recall bands playing, and many people, including soldiers out in the street. I was later told that this was the actual outbreak of war. I don't remember a great deal of my life in the orphanage, but aged five or six, I was moved from the children's home to the home for boys where my two elder brothers were. The leaving age in those days was 13, and those with no home to go to, were placed in work, usually as farm labourers. The parents of our matron, Miss Sargon, owned a farm at Conisborough, and I was fortunate, one summer, to spend the greater part of my holiday there in the company of another boy from the home.

Most of the summer holidays were spent in a camp on a farm on the outskirts of Leeds, living and sleeping under canvas, the field where we had our tents being immediately behind Lawnswood Cemetery. We always seemed to have lovely weather in those long ago summers, and hour after hour we wandered happily around the countryside.

I remember the nights when we lay with heads jutting out beneath the canvas of the tents, watching searchlights seeking out zeppelins over Ilkley Moor. We never saw any but were fascinated by the bright swathe of light sweeping across the sky.

Had it not been for the rationing of food we would not have known that there was a war on. It did not strike me as unusual that we three brothers neither received guests nor visited our relatives, as most of the other boys did. We accepted it as the result of our father living so far away. In consequence he was a complete stranger to us, and although we knew we had an older sister and two older brothers, we never saw or heard from them.

Attendance at morning church and afternoon Sunday school was of course obligatory. Although the orphanage was operated by the Quakers, we attended a Congregational Church and Sunday school. I never thought to inquire why, until I returned as a visitor some thirty years later but at that time I was not even curious.

One morning, returning from church, I noticed a man leaning on a cycle in the quadrangle. As we made to enter the building he motioned for me to approach him, but not knowing him, I hesitated until my oldest brother, Sydney said "We had better go and see what he wants — it's our father".

I would be about six years old and this was the first time that I had seen him for over four years. When you were poor in those days you really were poor, and my father could not afford the train journey from Blackburn to Leeds to visit his children.

Even on this occasion he had cycled over the Pennines to come and see us. I have no further recollections of the visit, and it was not until 1919, when the war had ended, that I saw him again. Then it was to tell us that he was going to remarry, and that we should be going back to Blackburn to live.

When I read and hear about poverty in England today I am often inclined to be cynical. The so-called poor and poverty stricken of today are unable to understand the meaning of the term.

This does not mean that in the orphanage we had not sufficient to eat, but there was certainly no super-abundance of food. We often knew what it was to go to bed hungry, particularly during the war years, but there was no similarity between the orphanage where I spent my childhood and Dotheboys Hall. The discipline was fairly strict, but laced with love and kindness, and memories of those years remain happy. I was a voracious reader taking whatever comics and boys books came my way and even on occasions the hardback adventure story.

The first hardback that I remember reading was "The Last of the Mohicans", by Fenimore Cooper, followed by "From Herat to Kabul" by G.A. Henty. We were encouraged to attend the local branch of The Band of Hope. Most of us attended, although it was not compulsory, the main stimulus being the occasional lantern-slide programme. We were also encouraged to read the Bible, and if we memorised particular Psalms and were able to recite them from memory, we were given a commemorative Bible to keep. I still have mine and make occasional use of it.

One of the few memorable incidents was being taken in a party to watch a cricket match at Headingly. I think it must have been shortly after the end of the war probably early in 1919. I remember little about the play but the two greatest cricketers of the day were both in action Jack Hobbs and Yorkshire's own George Hirst.

Another was when I paid my first visit to a Roman Catholic Church. I was taken, together with some of the other boys, at Christmas time to see the Nativity Crib in the Cathedral. I had never seen candles in a church before, and had always associated candles with going to bed, but the most significant memory was of the unusual and peculiar smell. I rather liked it and in later years was to become quite familiar with it. It was of course the smell of incense, but like many other things which used to distinguish the Catholic Church from its separated brethren it has now been down-played by Pope John's Ecumenism.

In the later years of the war there was the constant sight of hundreds of wounded soldiers in hospital blue wandering around Becket's Park, where I think there was a large wartime hospital. And finally the Victory celebration in Roundhay Park, the grand finale of which was a tableaux presentation of the Battle of Jutland with much sounding of cannon and clouds upon clouds of blue smoke. I was not a lover of war after that, although it did not make me a pacifist, but this again might have influenced my future attitude in later years.

It would be about this time that we had the second visit from my father. He arrived by train, bringing a lady with him, who he introduced as his future wife. She had worked at the same place of business as my father, and had already met my sister and two older brothers. This then was the opportunity for her to meet the rest of her intended husband's children.

It must have been a daunting experience for her, but she carried it off with little embarrassment and a show of expectant kindness, which the years did nothing but confirm. As stepmothers go she must have been one of the best, and we all missed her as a good friend when she died at the early age of fifty four.

The marriage took place in late June 1919, and early the following month we three brothers entrained for Blackburn and a new life. It was much later that I found out I had been born in Leeds, there for a short time father had a tailor's shop where he made and sold men's clothing. The other children had all been born in the adjoining small town of Batley, and this had been a contributory factor towards our acceptance into the Homes in Leeds.

Cliff Lane and Cliff Road were cul-de-sacs, the one ending in a high brick wall, the other with a pair of ornamental iron gates on the opposite side of which was a large garden and an imposing house. This was occupied by a Mr. and Mrs. Gibson and they always travelled about in a well-appointed Hansom cab of the apron front type.

Mrs. Gibson was one of the governors of the Homes and quite often she would make unexpected visits. She was very kind and often made us gifts of sweets or chocolates. Mr. Gibson was in business as a leather tanner, with a tannery at the bottom of a terraced hillside abutting their garden. It was possible to reach this terraced hillside called "The Ridge" by traversing two long passageways between high walls which we called 'ginnels'. Abutting the factory was a main road leading into the town centre called, I think, Meanwood Road.

There was another elderly lady who was also a governor, Miss Whiteside. Occasionally she would take me to church with her (not the congregational Church we normally attended) on a Sunday morning and regale me with sweets, often rum-flavoured. I recognised the taste later in life. The Quaker connection was maintained every Christmas by the distribution of chocolate drops from Terry's of York and Rowntree's Pastilles. Both of the families were Quakers. Every new Year's Day we each received a new penny.

So ended the first chapter of my life. On arrival in Blackburn we were pitchforked into a ready-made family with a mother and father whom we did not know, and two additional brothers and a sister all of whom were as shy and embarrassed as we.

On reflection they were happy days and I owe a debt of gratitude to those big-hearted and kindly people who gave me a home when I needed one.

When I stayed at the Sargon's farm they gave me a kitten, and I took it with me to Blackburn, living to a good age. I have always had at least one cat, except during the days when I was in Southampton, and of course during my sojourn in prison. I even had one in the camp at Peel, and my present cat is sitting on my knees as I type.

We were met at Blackburn station by my father, stepmother and sister. I naturally had no recollection of ever having seen her before, but she was very affectionate in her greeting and I knew immediately that we would become friends.

My father was not an affectionate man, at least not to his children, and I was somewhat overwhelmed by his presence, although he was trying, in his rather inhibited manner, to be friendly.

My sister immediately held me close in her arms and this itself was a new experience. I had only known officials of the orphanages and domestic employees, and although their treatment was always kind, physical expressions of affection were unknown.

We walked across a wide expanse called The Boulevard, and boarded a tram. After a mile we left it and walked a short distance to the terraced house where my father and my new family lived, the pattern of my life changed when I recommenced school in Blackburn.

In 1919 the textile industry which was the mainspring of employment in the town was fairly prosperous. There were hundreds of cotton mills perpetually belching smoke into the atmosphere and laying the foundation for the pollution problems of today. The country was experiencing the first post-war boom and little discontent or dissatisfaction was to be seen among the mass of the working population. Housing conditions were poor. Very few of the homes of the workers had a bath, or an indoor toilet. Hygiene was very elementary and toilet facilities in the factories were appalling, but little discontent was ever shown. The trade unions were never an influential force in the cotton towns of Lancashire. Even when the General Strike came in 1926 the textile workers did not come out on strike.

Clogs and shawl were the almost universal attire for the women who worked in the mills, and they actually represented the bulk of the workforce although many men were also employed. Social life was almost nonexistent. It was a five and a half day a week, from 7.45 a.m. until 5.30 p.m., with a break of one hour for lunch. There were no official tea-breaks, and the concept of 'master and men, of mistress and maidservant, of the rich man in his castle and the poor man at his gate' was so indelibly imprinted on the consciousness of the masses, that thought of change, the possibility of the worker emerging from the chrysalis of apparent stagnation, appeared to be beyond the dreams of even the wildest of philosophical thinkers.

My sister Isabel and two older brothers Alfred and Oswyn were awaiting our arrival. I had never known an Oswyn before or since, and he later dropped this little-known Saxon name in favour of his second name, Vincent. I remember little of those first weeks in Blackburn, but shortly after thoughts turned towards my schooling.

I had become an example of what would now be called ecumenism. My father had been a Wesleyan, my mother a Primitive Methodist, my early years had been spent under the protective care of the Quakers, I had attended a Congregational church on Sundays, while my early school days were spent at a Church of England Day school.

My father's second wife was a Roman Catholic, and he became a convert, sending me to a Catholic School and later having me baptised into the Catholic Faith. I still profess to being a Roman Catholic, albeit not a very good one.

My new school, St. Alban's High Grade was quite small, with only five classrooms and 150 pupils, under the head-mastership of Mr. Douthwaite, who was also the choir master of the adjacent church.

In those days each class had one teacher, who taught all subjects, and got to know personally the twist and quirk of personality and character of every student. There was greater rapport between teachers and pupils, particularly if the teacher was dedicated to his profession as most of them were.

It was more of a vocation than a money-earning profession. Respect for the teacher was automatic and generally speaking discipline was consonant with respect and obedience, although on occasion boisterous behaviour would take its toll and the natural ebullience of youth made itself evident.

My father (who had previously met the Head, to be made cognisant of my background) presented me to the Headmaster and made his exit. For the first time in my life I felt, and indeed was, completely on my own. The day passed without incident and I remember very little of it. On subsequent days I had to walk to school, home for dinner, walk back to school and at the end of the school day walk home again,

Shortly after going to St. Alban's I became aware that my singing voice was better than average. It did not take me long to learn hymns which were sung every morning before the start of lessons, and after only a few months the Headmaster gave me a

The author age 12

letter to take home for my father requesting permission for me to join the Church Choir.

To my deep regret he would not allow me to accept, arguing that it would entail Sunday attendance not only at the main morning Mass of the day, but also at the evening service of Benediction. I could not follow the logic of his reasoning because I would in any case be attending morning and evening service at our own parish church of St. Peters, at which adjacent school my brother was also in attendance.

However, my father's decisions never allowed for argument, and although I resented it, I found it wise in the long term to accept.

I had to contain mounting resentments over many years, but argument only earned retribution and a quiet tongue often avoided reprimand. When I informed the Head of my father's decision he looked at me somewhat askance and said "How strange". Many years later when faced with a similar situation he said "I am not surprised".

One thing however did give me satisfaction. I experienced no difficulty in always gaining good marks in the end-of-term examinations, rarely finishing below the first three in my class. I had been moved into a higher form only three months after starting at the school.

In 1921 the Government introduced the eleven-plus exam for all school attenders, and as this was also the year of the school-leaving age being raised to fourteen, the 14 year olds were also included along with the 11-13 year olds. A few weeks before the exams I badly scalded my foot and had been off school missing the special coaching laid on for those competing.

I don't know how many children there were in Blackburn in these four age groups but when the results were published I was fifty-first in grading.

I was naturally highly delighted, and was confident that I would be placed for entry into Preston Catholic College. I was, but to my bitter disappointment my father would not sanction acceptance. Although my form master and the headmaster tried to dissuade him, coming together to our home to present their arguments, it was all to no avail.

My father said that it was a question of cost, but the parents of other boys whom I knew and who agreed for their sons to go were no better off financially than my parents. I knew that finance was only an excuse, and I never did discover the real reason for his refusal, nor did he ever express any regret.

I was not to be treated in any way different from the other children of the family and apparently to his way of thinking this attitude prevented any suggestion of jealousy among my brothers and my sister. All I ever received from any of them were condolences for my misfortune. Unfortunately this event resulted in a stifling of ambition in the educational field, and although I continued to maintain my position in term accolades I made no particular effort for any exceptional achievement.

I enjoyed my school days in Blackburn and was sorry when the time came to leave. My elder brother — now called Peter — had left school two years before and was working in a cotton mill as a weaver. By this time the cotton trade was beginning to feel the first effects of the post-war slump, and mills were closing all over Lancashire.

My 14th birthday was approaching and with it the end of my schooldays. A few weeks before the close of that last term, my form master asked me what I intended for my future. I could only reply that my father had not disclosed his plans. I was soon to learn what those plans were, and with them the destruction of all hopes and dreams. After an abortive attempt by my great uncle David to have me apprenticed as a stableboy jockey — I had always been small and underweight for my age — my father informed me that he had decided I should start work in a cotton mill.

This came as a devastating shock not only to me, but to the rest of the family. But as always parental ruling brooked no opposition, but when I passed the news on to my teachers they were very angry.

After all this time it is difficult to understand my father's reasoning. My school reports over four and a half years had been excellent, although I had never been allowed to see them. Years later I was given a sight of my final report . . . "a boy of marked ability" ... "a boy deserving of every encouragement".

Both Head and form master had assured my father that I would easily gain my Matriculation — the great achievement of junior education at the time — and they did not accept defeat, using their influence with their families to get me an indentured position with either a local banker or accountant.

Despite the fact that these handsome arrangements would not have required the payment of any premium, my father again said no. They went away baffled and dismayed, my father telling them, "Give me credit for knowing what's best for my son's future". When I questioned him he simply told me not to be insolent.

And so I said my farewells to teachers and school friends, and in the New Year of 1924 started my working life in a cotton mill as a learner-weaver.

From the first day I hated it, as did my brother Peter who had already endured two years of the drudgery. It was to be another three years before we finally escaped.

The majority of the mills were operated as separate units, although many had a share capital. Amalgamations and asset stripping had not yet reared their head, although the pattern of financing the mushroom growth of the cotton mills of Madras, Bombay, and Calcutta by the City of London was beginning to make itself felt by the end of 1921.

By 1923 the Indian Dhooty, a type of thin muslin which had been the "bread and butter" of much of Lancashire's trade, had already been transferred to India's sweat shops. The first instance of British capital from the City being used to undercut the home product with consequent unemployment. As the mills of Lancashire began to close, asset stripping emerged and the actual looms from the Lancashire mills were dismantled, transported to India, and reassembled. I actually witnessed this process taking place until I left Blackburn in 1927. It was the constant reiteration of these happenings by my father, around the table at meal time, which first introduced me to the basic factors of finance and economics.

Now came the General Strike of 1926, and although the textile workers were not involved, mills continued to close. During this period tea-table talk became increasingly concerned with economics and political theory. Robert Blatchford was the journalistic political pundit of his day and his constant reappraisal of the economic situation was absorbed with my daily bread.

My father's family, had for a time, lived in Rochdale, the birthplace of the Co-operative movement, with which at one time my father had sympathy. In his early years of young manhood he had come into contact with, and had on occasion met, the early leaders of the socialist movement. Names like Jimmy Maxton, Philip Snowden and J.R. Clynes were often quoted not only as names but as persons actually known. My political education was now in process of development. I was not encouraged to interject but I was an avid listener and had an absorbent memory.

The mill where Peter was working closed, and he was now out of work. There was virtually no hope of finding alternative work in textiles, and he joined Syd and Vin in Southport, where he soon found employment on the Pleasure Beach as a "barker" and fare collector on the multiplicity of roundabouts operated by an amusement caterer.

The future now looked very bleak to me. The two brothers of my childhood years had now left and the age gap of eight years between myself and Alf was too great for there to be much in common — plus the fact that he was now contemplating marriage.

For three years I had been attending the local technical college studying the design and management sides of cotton textiles, and although I absorbed the techniques and general basics, there was no true desire to become proficient because at heart I hated the whole concept of a life in textiles, an industry which anyway seemed to have no future in the post-war world.

I was now seventeen, and had begun to appreciate the company of the opposite sex. I remember the first girl I ever kissed, and the pleasurable pulsing of the loins which accompanied it. Her name was Josephine, and she was my age. I used to carry her books home from night school. But these were only spasmodic interludes. I was becoming increasingly dissatisfied with my lot in life and constantly chafed against parental restriction and control. My behaviour was becoming rebellious and my father was slowly becoming aware of the brewing storm.

One evening, without any preamble, he said, "Is there any other kind of work which you would like to do? I know we can't put the clock back as if you were just leaving school but think about it and let me know." For a moment I was stunned. This was a father whom I had not previously known. Perhaps the future was not irretrievably black.

My stepmother was a good cook and pastry and cake maker, and for many years I had willingly helped her. I already had two brothers in the baking trade, they appeared to be happy in their work, and so I told my father I wished to become a baker.

Fortunately he had a business acquaintance who was in the business and within weeks I had left the mill and was working as a baker's junior. Although the hours were long and the wages very small for a boy of seventeen, life held new hope. I even began to sing again, something I hadn't done for many years, and my stepmother had noticed it. I like to think that she was the ultimate softening influence in the attitude of my father. He and I never became close, but I eventually came to accept that perhaps at the time he did what he thought was right.

I was eager to learn and in addition to my job I attended nightly bakery school to speed up my skills. I also joined the Bakery Students Society and found that I was not inhibited from speaking in front of others. I had been a keen debater at school and had thoroughly enjoyed play readings, particularly those of Shakespeare, and easily committed long tracts to memory, in some of which I am still word perfect today.

In the early summer of 1927 my brother arranged an interview for me in Southport with his employer. He was already a foreman baker with the firm of James Willman, a good class bakery and confectionery business, and after a short interview Mr. Williams agreed to take me on. I served a week's notice with my Blackburn employer, packed my few possessions into a hold-all and sped as fast as the train would take me to Southport.

How can anyone know what it is like to be free unless they have first been denied freedom? In later life I was to experience prison life, but at the time my joy knew no bounds.

After settling into lodgings with my brother, I went down on to the beach and ran, and ran, until I collapsed from exhaustion, almost overcome with my first experience of *Joie de vivre*.

The work was hard and the wages low, but work itself was sheer joy. My wages were twenty-five shillings per week, and lodgings cost (including three meals per day) eighteen shillings, compulsory laundry for work, another one shilling and sixpence, leaving five shillings and sixpence per week for clothing and entertainment.

I thought these happy days would continue indefinitely, but

nemesis was again lurking in the wings ready to deliver his blow. The Depression and the collapse of the American stock market was only 12 months away, and interest rates in Britain were starting to climb. My employer had built a new bakery on borrowed money, and with the seasonal drop in trade, decided to cut staff. I was axed, and with no unemployment benefit, returned beneath my parental roof.

Although I did not stay long, I took advantage of my time to polish up my ballroom dancing, finding unpaid work, but with free admittance, as a steward at a local dance hall. Shortly after I began work bread-making with The Corner House Cafe Ltd in Blackburn, a job which also gave me an opportunity to develop my wider skills. Although I sometimes worked unbelievably long hours I never regretted my move. In an eight-day period covering that August Bank Holiday of 1929, I worked almost 113 hours with eighteen and a half hours sleep. Occasionally we would go to one of the many theatres or to a dancing session at the Winter Gardens Ballroom or Tower Ballroom where Reginald Dixon would play the Wonder Wurlitzer Organ, and Victor Sylvester gave his early dancing demonstrations.

My time in Blackburn was more than enjoyable, and had developed my professional skills considerably. But after six months, my seasonal contract came to an end, and aged 20 was once more back in Southport, unemployed. In my absence the Palladium Cinema had been razed to the ground in a fire and then rebuilt, while the old Opera House, rebuilt after a similar incident, had been renamed the Garrick Theatre.

My brother Sydney introduced me to the live stage, both plays and light entertainment. I remember seeing and hearing Gracie Fields. This was while she was still married to her first husband Archie Pitt. A cat-call from "The Gods", during an intercession in the programme asked "Where's Archie?". (There were already rumours of a break in the marriage). Quick as a flash Gracie replied, "He's doing what you are not doing, minding his own business". Her reply brought the house down.

Other names I recall seeing in that period were Florrie Ford, Gertie Gitana, Harry Champion (also a Mosleyite), Little Tich, and Sir Harry Lauder, all of who appeared at the Old Opera House. The Opera House was part of The Winter Garden complex, comprising in addition The Scala Cinema, a skating rink, and a small menagerie, all within extensive ornamental gardens surrounded by a wall.

There were at the time about nine or ten cinemas in Southport among them the Palladium, the Coliseum, the Palace, the Trocadero, the Picturedrome, the Savoy (which later became the Regent), the Bedford, and the Birkdale Palace. The Picturedrome, which was on Lord Street and had been Southport's first cinema, was pulled down and is now an open space. I once tried to buy it for conversion into a skating rink, but was refused planning permission.

The Trocadero was converted into Woolworths, the Palladium was knocked down and in its place was erected Sainsburys. The Scala was also demolished and partly replaced by the Kingsway. The Regal, when I last drove past appeared to be closed but the Palace was re-named the Classic and I think is now Southport's last cinema. The Grand is perhaps a post-war building, certainly built after I left Southport in 1935, and is now a Bingo Hall, as is also the once elegant Garrick Theatre. So much for progress? The skating rink was an early casualty and on its site now stands The Tudor Bar.

Early in the New Year I wrote to my old Blackpool firm asking when I could expect to resume work, but to my dismay was told that it had gone into voluntary liquidation. It was suggested that there might be better job prospects down south, and after some inquiries I found work in Hampshire, at Romsey, a few miles from Southampton.

I said my adieus to brother Sydney, not without misgivings, and after travelling all day, arrived at the cafe-restaurant in the village square. There I met my new employer, a Mr. Turner, and after a light meal, was taken to meet my landlady. She turned out to be elderly, married and rather starch-faced, nothing like the one I had left in Southport, who in the years to come was to prove not only a very good friend, but almost a surrogate mother. My lodgings were sparse indeed, a small room with cold lino on the floor and a dormer window. Although this was March, there was no form of heating. I was not encouraged to leave my room except for an evening meal, and overall life did not look very bright.

Fortunately on that first Sunday the sun shone. I went to church in the morning, visited Romsey Abbey and wandered around the grounds, and at eight the next morning presented myself at the shop. My employer was already there and informed me that all his bakery products were handmade including the bread. I had never made bread by hand in large quantities, only very small amounts at home for home consumption.

It was his practise to make bread from "overnight dough", a technique I knew from my studies at the bakery school but had never used. The principle was to make a dough from water well below blood temperature, using only a small amount of yeast. This created a very slow fermentation. The dough was then allowed to stand overnight, then weighed-off and moulded into various shapes and sizes. The slow-fermenting process was supposed to produce a good eating loaf with a slow-staling process.

To the best of my knowledge it is never used today mainly because it was too slow and time-consuming and also because the method did not blend in with modern plant processing methods. It was fairly common in the Thirties. What amazed me on this occasion however was not so much the method as the quantity made in the one exercise. I thought that I had worked hard in Blackpool. Blackpool was a kindergarten compared to Romsey.

I remained with Mr. Turner for only a few weeks, and shortly after took up part-time work in nearby Southampton. I found congenial lodgings quite close to my new bakery in a side street off the Shirley Road, but after becoming unemployed once more, moved to a bed-sitter. My living conditions now were very frugal, and my room cost twelve shillings and sixpence out of dole money that had been cut to eighteen shillings and sixpence.

I often knew what it was to go hungry, but fortunately my land-lady was not hard-hearted, and often provided me with a hot meal when I returned from Mass on Sunday. It was during this period in 1931 that I read Oswald Mosley's resignation speech in the Sunday Express, taking his leave of a Labour Government that had failed to deal with the unemployment problem it had been put into power to resolve.

A month or so later I received a visitor, a friend from a nearby bakery, a fellow Yorkshireman, who was trying to do two jobs and slowly undermining his health in the process. He made me a proposition which I could not turn down. I was to go and live with his family and be treated as such, and in return I would do what baking was necessary at night to supply his own business. I would not receive any cash wages but could continue to draw my seventeen shillings (now reduced to fifteen shillings and threepence) dole as my own without any outgoings.

By working a few hours each night I was still available for employment, and as I did not receive any wages I was not drawing unemployment benefit unlawfully. This arrangement was to continue so long as both sides remained in agreement.

For me the situation was ideal. I had a home, good food, and unlimited time to seek alternative employment if I so desired. It was also agreed that if and when the business could pay me a wage in addition to food and lodging this would be done.

During this period I took up ice skating, but did not become as proficient as I had on rollers. I also became a regular attender at "The Saints" Dirt Track, and was an avid follower of their fortune in the Speedway Calender. At the time, the captain of the team was the World Champion rider Jack Parker and also included his brother Norman and the Swedish rider Morian Hansen. I came to know them well and was often in the pits between races.

It was also during this period that I was asked to join the choir of St. Boniface Church, and singing became again one of the great joys of my life.

I also attended Quarr Abbey on the Isle of Wight. This was a Benedictine Monastery and Benedictine monks were noted for their particular aptitude in the rendering of early church music known as Plain or Gregorian Chant. We went as a choir for tuition and for the sheer joy of listening to the monks during a sung mass. This music possesses a haunting lilt which penetrates the soul and captivates the ear.

Occasionally we are treated to a television broadcast from a monastery in one of the Sunday programmes and I am back in time to Quarr Abbey and singing in time with the monastic brotherhood. Credo in Unam Deum, Patrem Omnipotentem, Factorem Caeli et terrae, Visibilium omnium, et invisibilium. I am still word-perfect after all these years. To me it is still the most beautiful music in the world.

I was also associated at this time with the Catholic lay societies, the Society of St. Vincent de Paul and the Knights of St.Columba.

I recall studying Rerum Novarum, the almost socialist encyclical of Pope Leo 13th. Its political significance was not to impress itself on me for a number of years, and I was concerned in the most personal interpretation of the better things of life. My response, when it came, demanded a commitment for life.

It was during the few years that I spent in Southampton that I

Author age 17 at Douglas, Isle of Man where 13 years later he was to suffer imprisonment without charge or trial.

became aware of the burgeoning rise of resentment and anger among the mass of the people, the result of rising unemployment. The final straw was the lowering of the unemployment benefit by 10% from 17 Shillings to 15 Shillings and 3 Pence per week. You could physically feel the animosity against the government in the dole queue. I write from first hand knowledge. I knew what it was to be hungry.

Government learned a lot from Oswald Mosley in the seven years from 1932 to 1939. They realised that if you grind the people down hard enough and long enough they will eventually rebel and will be ready to follow a man of integrity if he gives a resolute lead.

It is true that periodic visits to the workhouse and what I saw in that ghastly establishment prepared the basis of all my future political activity, but Mosley's resignation speech brought the culmination of my own political development. It must not be inferred from the foregoing that I am a deeply religious person. I am not. I have always been a 'Doubting Thomas', and although I might admire Thomas Aquinas, I was never anxious to step into either his shoes or his footsteps. My love of singing has always helped to bolster my faith, but now that I can no longer sing, where is my bolster? Do I still need one? I fear that I do.

So I continued to try to push my burgeoning political conscience into the background and concentrated on a spate of *joie de vivre*. My working time was pleasant and my spare time became fully occupied. Often after Sunday Mass I would join other members of the choir for a glass of beer and a game of 'Shove-halfpenny' at the Rising Sun, close to the Atherley Cinema, but Sunday afternoon often required my attendance at the local workhouse, distributing 2d packets of Woodbines, and ounces of tobacco.

Then in the Spring of 1932, brother Sydney wrote to tell me he had found a job for me back in Southport. I was happy in Southampton, but there were few prospects of advancement and still millions unemployed. So I took the gamble. I made my farewells to my 'Southampton family' and my numerous friends, both at the church and elsewhere, packed my bag and returned to Southport.

For the third time I came to live in the Lancashire resort, but alas the job soon turned out to be appalling, and I quickly found alternative work in a bakery in Churchtown on the outskirts of Southport, owned by a Mr. Halliwell, only a few hundred yards from the house where I now live. He proved to be the best employer I ever had. There were two girls employed in the bakery, one about my age, and one considerably younger. Her name was Edith Johnson, and she was to become my very dear wife, the most loyal that any man could wish for.

In the summer of 1932 I bought my first motor cycle, a barrel tank, two stroke, two speed BSA, capable of 37mph with a following wind, and purchased for 35 shillings. At that time Britain produced the finest bikes in the world, Norton, HRD, BSA, Ariel, Brough, Francis-Barnett, Rudge-Ulster, Cotton and Sunbeam, with the German BMW our only serious competitor.

As winter closed in, my brother and I decided to try and make some extra money running a dance club in a hired room at the Kingsway Cafe. We hired a dance band "Billie Atherton's Boys" and provided light refreshments, and although we did not make a fortune, it was worth the time and effort. Unfortunately the local council built the present Floral Hall and virtually put us out of business.

Life continued its pleasant pattern well into 1933, and in that sunshine summer I would finish my stint in early afternoon and swim in the sea-bathing lake with my brother, before leaving for a cafe-restaurant, and perhaps later a dance. And it was into this carefree world that Saturday evening that Tommy Moran stepped with his penny "Blackshirt" and with it the vision of the New World to be won.

Chapter Two

Blackshirt Brother

I stuffed the "Blackshirt" into my pocket and continued on my way to the dance. I didn't read it until the following morning, and my brother Sydney asked me what I had got. I told him it was the weekly paper of Mosley's movement. He read it, but passed no comment.

The address of the newly-opened local headquarters, rubber stamped on the front page was 51 Houghton Street, only a few minutes walk from where I lived and I decided to call there the following evening.

I was not very talkative the following day at work. I was recalling that Sunday in Southampton and my reading of Mosley's speech in the Sunday Express, my visits to the workhouse, charitable work which I had now opted out of. I was not even a regular church goer, although I can truthfully say I never became an unbeliever.

My political conscience was re-emerging from its hibernation, and at the time I really did not want it to. Life was very pleasant and enjoyable. I had read of the formation of Mosley's New Party, the forerunner of the British Union of Fascists: it was a general item of news at the time, but I had also read with some feelings of regret of its failure and debacle at the 1931 election.

Now, here was Mosley again. Intruding into my life at the most inopportune time. I was no longer on the dole. I had a good job which I liked. I had a good employer. I had a circle of very close friends. Was I wise in going to his local headquarters and putting it all at risk?

I knew myself sufficiently well even at that age to know that I was in danger of becoming committed. I went, and met the local Branch Officer, Harry Leslie Lyon Jones. How strange to remember his name so clearly! I even remember where he lived: No. 4 Park Road. He was unmarried, about thirty years old, lived with his widowed mother and was a commercial traveller for Dewar's Whisky.

I talked to him for more than two hours on that Monday evening. One of the questions I asked was whether Mosley's Movement was anti-Semitic. He replied that it was not, and indeed if I had been told otherwise, I would not have joined. Finally I signed an application form for membership.

When I got home my brother was getting ready for his night shift. When I told him that I had just joined British Union he looked at me somewhat quizzically and said, "I suppose it was to be expected. You always were a joiner".

He would often question me as to my reasons for joining and query the depth of my political conviction, but he continued to read the Blackshirt which I brought home each week.

Soon after, he lost his job with the firm that he had been with since his first arrival in Southport in 1925. There was still much unemployment and he soon realised that the prospects of finding alternative employment in the town were far from good, so he decided to join my brother Peter in Hull. Peter had been transferred from Louth to a shop recently opened by the same firm. So off he went and once again I was on my own.

The reaction of my friends to my political conversion was — to my very great surprise — non-commital. They were just rather surprised that John Charnley, who in the past had been concerned only with the "good things in life" should have dedicated himself to political activity. We all remained close friends right up to the day I left Southport in January 1935.

As I was to find out in the course of my life, the great majority of English people are not politically minded. The same applied in the 1930's as it does today. There was virtually no animosity in the earlier days of the Movement, unless it was shown at a big meeting when Communists came deliberately to cause trouble. Then, of course, you got a hooligan element which joined in. But the general mass of people were curious about Mosley; they were interested in him as a person, and in his policies, and if you could get a quiet meeting they listened, and were invariably enthusiastic.

In those first days in the autumn of 1933, I did not, however, become immediately dedicated to Mosley and British Union. This took place gradually over a period of months.

Mosley always contended that unless there was a total collapse of law and order — in which case he would place the Movement alongside the Forces of the Crown to bring about the restoration of stability — British Union's only path to power was through the ballot box. Although he believed the electoral system to be antiquated and unfairly weighted in favour of the status quo, he would never-the-less take advantage of the first-past-the-post voting system in order to bring about the re-organisation of Parliamentary government.

British Union proposed that the elected government should not rule for more than four years and that the power of the parties to frustrate the will of the people should be restricted. Despite this they would be allowed to propagate their idea from the public platform. At the end of the four years, the electorate would be asked by direct plebiscite to either approve or disapprove of the Government's record. In the event of a vote of censure, the Government would resign, and a General Election held in which all the parties would be permitted to participate, but this time under a revised system of proportional representation.

If the plebiscite backed the British Union Government, steps would be taken to introduce a system of government based

Blackshirt brothers. Peter, Alf, John and Sydney. Like John, Alf was to become a District Leader of Bolton, Lancashire.

on the concept of the Corporate State. Under this each major industry would have its own Corporation made up of representatives of employer, worker, and consumer. Trade union membership would be compulsory, and worker representation on the controlling body of the Corporation would be by election from the entire trade union membership within that industry. This, argued Mosley, was true democracy.

The Corporation would be responsible for wages and conditions of work, as well as having direct representation in a Government that would also include representatives from the armed forces, judiciary, the police, and the world of education, science, finance and so on.

This plan for a British Corporate State was the brain child of Raven Thomson, and was part of the most detailed and all-embracing political policy ever seen in this country. No British politician has produced such a detailed programme covering the whole spectrum of industry and agrarian life, as that advanced by Oswald Mosley between late 1932 and 1940. No matter what part of the country, or what industry, Mosley had a practical approach to the problem and a realistic solution for immediate implementation. If you were a miner for example, British Union Government would stop the export of British capital to overseas competitors, while controlling imports of coal.

Finance would be provided at low interest rates to produce more petrol from coal, boosting our mining industry and with it wages and working conditions of our miners, whilst at the same time reducing the level of petrol and crude oil imports. If you were a Hull docker handling timber imports, a Mosley Government would increase the demand for imported timber through its massive national house-building and slum clearance programme.

If you worked in cotton textiles it had to be accepted that while you would be unable to regain the Indian market for the cheaper product, you could protect the home market for the better quality product against foreign products financed by the City of London.

Are you involved in the fishing industry? Then set up the operation of factory ships for the extraction of oil from fish for use in the food trade and in animal feeding stuffs. The regeneration of industrial production automatically results in an uplift in the overall purchasing power which in turn creates further regeneration.

An upsurge in spending power would result in increased demand for consumer durables, and more and more cars from British car factories would be seen on our roads. British Union took a radical approach to our motorways, and we even had a booklet entitled 'Motorways of Britain', the first overall plan for dual and treble carriage ways to be seen in Europe, long before Hitler built his auto-bahn.

British agriculture was in a parlous state which appeared to grow progressively worse from the early 1920's. British industrial exports dominated the markets of the world because of low production costs linked to low wages. This could only be maintained by cheap food, 40% of which was imported, mainly from the Argentine, whose industries were dominated and in many instances owned outright by British capital.

To revitalise British agriculture would require an entire reorientation of thought. The concept of cheap food would have to be abandoned and a better return in the form of wages and profit for the worker and farmer adopted. This was to be done by introducing fresh capital at low interest rates, which would allow for modernisation of equipment and increased production, combined with some measure of protection against cheap foreign imports.

The general improvement in overall living standards from the revitalised industries would permit a raising of agricultural prices at market and retail level, with the entire economy benefiting from an ever increasing purchasing power and demand.

The shipping industry would also benefit by the restricting of British coastal shipping to British owned ships, not ships sailing under a British Flag of convenience.

This overall concept of economic nationalism could only be adopted and made viable within the orbit of a protected market area within the Empire. Once that viable area disappeared the entire concept would collapse. The realisation of this occurring in the event of war was one of the contributary clauses in the formation of our foreign policy which can be summarised as Britain First, Britain for the British, and keep out of foreign quarrels.

Some weeks after joining, I began giving up my Saturday dancing in order to sell the Blackshirt, usually on the site outside Woolworths where I had first seen Tommy Moran. Tommy was a staff member and a first-rate open-air platform speaker, and a man of rare courage. His work consisted of stimulating the growth of newly-formed branches by assisting in sales drives not only in the area of a new-branch but also in virgin territory.

He would make occasional visits to Southport, but since there were no authorised open-air speaking sites, and the local authority would not sanction open-air meetings, we would sometimes go to Ormskirk, the nearby market town, to hold a meeting. These were invariably held on the comer of Moor Street and Moorgate. In the meantime, I had read Mosley's book 'The Greater Britain', and this, together with my regular reading of the Blackshirt, had given me a basic knowledge of the policy of the Movement, supplemented by a pamphlet entitled 'Ten Points of Fascist Policy'.

Early in the new year of 1934, Mosley was billed to speak at the Stadium, Liverpool, and I and other Southport members attended as stewards. On that occasion, however, Mosley was down with some complaint which prohibited his attendance, and the meeting was addressed by William Joyce, later to become infamous during the war years as 'Lord Haw-Haw'.

It was the first time that I had heard Joyce speak. He was a brilliant speaker but had a vitriolic tongue when dealing with either interrupters or when in full spate against conditions or persons against which or whom he had an aversion.

I was to meet him often in later years and come to know him quite well. He was undeniably anti-semitic and this, together with his vicious tongue, may have detracted from his asset as a persuasive speaker. I was quite impressed with his performance on this occasion, and also remember another, on the steps of Leeds Town Hall when his vitriolic repartee almost led to a riot.

The meetings in Ormskirk were always held on Thursday, and I got into the habit of taking another Southport member with me

Most Yorkshire and Lancashire towns and cities had BUF branches in the 1930's. Here Bradford blackshirts, the young and not so young, the poor and not so poor march in 1934.

on my motorbike to assist in paper selling. I had, by now, become quite friendly with Tommy, who was an ex-rating, and a one-time middle-weight boxing champion of the Royal Navy. A most reassuring man to have at your side in the event of any fighting, as I was to find on many, many occasions!

Came a night in Ormskirk when Tommy turned to me as we were having our pre-meeting drink in the Queens Head and said, "Why don't you have a go?" I must confess I had always had a jealous admiration of a good speaker and now here was my chance. While at school I had often done Shakespearian play reading, and had been complimented on my delivery and style. Even as a schoolboy I found that I had a natural ability to use gestures and mannerisms, and my master had told me on one occasion that I had the makings of an orator.

I was, however, very hesitant and Tommy realising how nervous I was said, "Do you know why you joined the Movement?" I replied "Of course I do", to which he said: "Then get up and say so, you only need to speak for five minutes, but before you get down, tell them that you are only introducing the speaker". We left the pub, carrying our beer box which we used as a makeshift platform, set it down on the wide footpath opposite the pub and after some encouragement I made my debut as a public speaker.

The first few moments were frightening, with my stomach doing somersaults. It then settled down, and to my amazement I found that I was a natural. Public speaking was a thing to be enjoyed!

The spring of 1934 saw the launching by the B.U.F. of 'The Cotton Campaign', a concentration of publicity and Leader's Meetings programmed to direct attention to the mounting collapse of cotton textiles. Mills all over Lancashire continued to close, and more and more British capital was being invested in mills in Bombay, Madras and Calcutta, where production costs were only fractional when compared with those of Lancashire.

The campaign was given a send-off with a packed meeting at Manchester's Free Trade Hall, and I travelled with a complement of Southport members to assist in the stewarding of the meeting. There were to be a series of marches from differing points and timed to arrive at the Hall about 6.30p.m. The doors were to be opened to the public half an hour later, and Mosley was due to address the meeting at 8.0 pm.

It was his custom to have a small table and a microphone in the centre of the platform. There would be no other person on the platform either before the start of the meeting or during the main speech, which would usually last an hour-and-a-half, throughout which he never referred to notes.

His continuity and flow of rhetoric was phenomenal. He would quote facts, figures and economic data without the slightest hesitation. His speeches were always divided into three parts, beginning with an examination of the problem (depending on the main theme of his address), proceeding to his proposals, and/or solution, followed with a peroration of pulsating dynamism. This was the first time that I had heard him speak and I was completely bowled over, fascinated, and imbued with an inner feeling of spiritual uplift. Over the years I was to hear him hundreds of times and he never failed to uplift me.

At the conclusion of a typical meeting, Mosley would mingle with the crowd, many of whom he would know personally, and chat. He had a remarkable memory for names. Some time later, when I was living in Hull he paid a visit to our branch headquarters, before going on to an open air meeting at Corporation Fields. At our offices I introduced him to a docker, George Badger, who'd been in the Army in the First War. The following year Oswald Mosley spoke in Hull again, and seeing George in the ranks, went across and spoke to him. When the meeting was over George came up to me and said, 'John, he even knew my name, and I've only met him once!'

There were a number of district headquarters in Manchester and each contingent of visiting stewards was instructed where to report in readiness for the programmed marches. The Southport members had to report to an address in Cheetham Hill and on arrival we were provided with a cup of tea.

While we were awaiting to move off we heard that a party of Blackshirts, heading for our rendezvous, had been waylaid and attacked in a nearby street. Not appreciating that we were in unfamiliar territory, I, and two other Southport members, George Bodosian and Noni McCarthy, set off to find them and assist in the scrimmage. Bodosian's father was a naturalised Armenian, who had fled from the terrors of persecution in that troubled area shortly after the First World War, and McCarthy was of Irish parentage, his parents having been a one-time dual turn of the music halls, known in their day as 'Noni and McCarthy'.

By the time we arrived the scrimmage was over, the Blackshirts had got safely away, and we three had run into trouble! It was the first time, but not the last, that I had been involved in a street fight. I have always been small, my weight then about nine stone.

It happened so quickly: one minute we were racing towards this congestion of people, and as we arrived on the outskirts of the crowd they opened up and we realised that we were the only Blackshirts there and were completely surrounded by a hostile crowd.

I suddenly felt a severe blow to the head and that I was on the ground. Then I was literally picked up by my legs and arms and thrown through a plate glass shop window. At the sound of the crashing glass the crowds ceased their attack and rapidly disappeared down the side streets. I realised later that they were afraid I had suffered severe injuries.

I found myself lying on my back on the window boards of what I assumed to be a butcher's shop. On either side of me was a potted geranium in full bloom, and in front was a huge gash in the shop window.

My companions were coming towards me and there was no one else in sight. With great care I climbed out of the smashed window, amazed to find that I was not in any way injured, although feeling very sore and bruised.

The only visible evidence of the escapade was a slight gash in my uniform belt and this undoubtedly had saved me from a serious back wound, otherwise I was not even scratched. We wasted no time in returning to our assembly point for our march into the city. I thought little more of the event at the time although it was to have repercussions and a surprising sequel. The uniform belt lies on the table before me as I type this recounting of the most dramatic episode of my early Blackshirt days.

Later that week two policemen visited our headquarters and asked to see John Charnley. The owner of the shop had claimed from his insurers for replacement costs and they in turn were seeking financial recompense from the person who had broken the window.

It raised a fine legal point. Was I responsible, or the persons who had thrown me through the window? If a window is broken by a brick, is the brick responsible or the person who threw the brick? I gave my version of the occurrence and this was substantiated by my two companions, and Harry Jones assured the police that if a claim for damages was preferred against me we would defend any such claim. The police left and I heard no more about the affair. I would have thought no more about it had it not been for the eventual sequel.

A few weeks later as part of the same campaign I was again attending a Leader's Meeting in Burnley. Before the meeting I was told that Mosley wished to see me afterwards. I was somewhat perturbed and thought I was to be reprimanded for foolish behaviour in leading other members into an unnecessary street fight.

When the meeting ended and Mosley had retired to a private room, I was sent for. I knocked on the door and the now-familiar voice called to me come in. He was sitting at a table with a glass of water. I walked to the table, saluted him in the customary fashion and stood to attention. Even to write of this episode after fifty years still fills me with emotion. He asked me to briefly outline what had occurred, and this I did. Then he stood up, looked at me with those penetrating eyes, which seemed to be alive with electrifying sparks, shook me vigorously by the hand and said, "Charnley, I need men like you".

From that moment I have been his man, and I shall remain so always. When, in December 1980 the news of his death was announced on the morning television news I was at my place of business in Ormskirk, and one of the partners called me to the phone. It was my wife to tell me that Oswald Mosley had died at his home in France. I did not say much but when I put the phone down I must have shown my sense of shock. "Has somebody died?" I was asked. "Yes", I replied, "a very dear friend. I shall miss him sorely as long as I live".

I was now devoting more and more of my time to the Movement, and improving my ability as a speaker. Consequently I saw less and less of my friends. They never criticised my political commitment but could not reconcile it with my previous pattern of behaviour. We still had our card sessions in my flat if I was not away at a Leader's Meeting, but they realised that this was not to be a flash in the pan but something I had accepted as part of my life.

The Ormskirk meetings were now a regular feature of my weekly programme and as I shall recount later I must have made some lasting impressions.

During the early part of this campaign Mosley addressed a meeting in Southport at the Floral Hall. Being a holiday resort, Southport was not expected to produce a rowdy meeting, and the audience was quiet and attentive. For some reason which I never learned, there had not been the customary blaze of pre-meeting advertising. The usual procedure was to use the public hoardings with a head and shoulders of Mosley with folded arms and a semi-profile head held at a slightly uplifted angle on a background of crossed flags and carrying the simple statement 'Mosley Speaks' with the time and place of meeting.

Only a few of these posters appeared and I was concerned at the lack of publicity. As propaganda was now my department I felt responsible and hit upon a solution. On the Saturday before the meeting, I would repeatedly tour the town on my motor bike with a suitably inscribed poster on my back, in the nature of mobile 'sandwich man'.

One of our members who had a flair for this work prepared the poster which was pasted on a sheet of hardboard and securely strapped to my back and off I went on my tour. I kept as close to the kerb as I reasonably could, and only travelled in low gears. It was a huge success and created something of a sensation in the town centre, particularly as I was doing a continuous tour, and wearing my Blackshirt uniform.

After about half an hour I was flagged down by a policeman who, obviously acting on instructions, told me that I was probably breaking the law and advised me not to continue. I asked him what law I was breaking and when he could not tell me I replied that I intended to continue. On my next ride down Chapel Street four uniformed policemen, two from each side of the road prevented my driving by. One was a sergeant who warned that if I continued I would be arrested and charged with "Obstructing the police in the execution of their duty".

If I had been as belligerent then as I was later to become I would have defied them and courted arrest, knowing that the resultant publicity would have become nationwide, but at the time I felt that I owed some loyalty to my employer, and agreed to discontinue my publicity campaign. I was told however, that I would probably be charged with an offence under a section of the local bylaw, and my poster was confiscated as evidence.

The meeting took place the following day and was packed, the Movement gaining quite a few new recruits the following week. I was surprised to see my employer in the audience, and noted that on occasions he applauded with some enthusiasm. He had in the past, obliquely referred to my activities in the political field, but always in a tolerant manner and I was careful never to introduce politics into any conversation with any member of the staff. He once asked me why I joined and I told him it was because England had many problems and that only Oswald Mosley appeared to have any answers.

Some weeks later an event occurred for which I was solely responsible, causing my employer considerable embarrassment. Churchtown was still very much a village community with a heavily-voiced village conscience. The result was that I was asked to leave. My employer did not want to part with my services and I certainly did not wish to lose my job, but village protocol decided otherwise, and I was again out of work. We parted company with sincere regrets on both sides and an assurance from my ex-employer that he would always willingly give help or advise should I ever ask for it. This I did on two future occasions, once when I required a qualifications reference, when seeking work on my return from the Isle of Man in January 1944, and again in 1946 when contemplating buying a bakery business in nearby Burscough Bridge.

I was now faced with a financial problem. Reduced once more to the dole subsistence level, I could no longer maintain the cost of my flat, but Harry Jones suggested a possible temporary solution.

Shortly before Mosley's meeting at the Floral Hall, we had moved our headquarters into much larger premises, the top floor of a three-storey building in Neville Street, above a large garage. The premises were quite extensive, comprising toilet and washroom facilities, a well-appointed kitchen, two large rooms, one of which we fitted out with a bar and much used as a lounge and club room. Another large room was used for various types of physical training including fencing at which I tried my hand, not with a great deal of success. There was also a smaller room, which had been converted to an administrative office.

The proposal was that if I could provide my own sleeping facilities I could bed down in the office whilst ensuring that no visible evidence cluttered the office during the day, use the kitchen for the preparation of my meals, and act as a resident caretaker. My landlady gave me my bed-chair which I had been using in my flat and I moved in.

As a temporary measure it was quite satisfactory, although I new that I could not accept it as a permanency. I was beginning to feel like a piece of flotsam on the surface of a sea which could become too rough in those unsettled times. It did, however, provide a temporary solution which accommodated me for about three months.

Some time later I received a summons to attend the Court of Summary Jurisdiction to answer a charge of contravention of a local bylaw. When I attended the Court I was charged with 'Driving a mechanically-propelled vehicle on the King's Highway for an unlicensed purpose', to which I pleaded guilty, my objective being to get away with as small a fine as possible.

In my defence I quoted a number of known instances where other vehicles including transport operated by the local council were in breach of the same bylaw, citing specific instances such as advertising posters for various functions, some held in the same council owned building, where we had held Mosley's meeting. The chairman of the magistrates bnished this aside and refused to accept it as exoneration. I was found guilty and fined a pound.

It was obvious that it had already been decided that I was to be found guilty, and I found out later that there was no such offence as that under which I had been charged. There were two classified breaches of the transport law,one 'Driving without due consideration for other road users', and 'Dangerous Driving', and under neither of these could I be charged. From that day my belief in Britain Justice was minimal.

In the September of that year I had attended a Leader's Meeting at Leeds Town Hall. To my utter amazement I saw my three brothers all wearing the Blackshirt. When Sydney had arrived in Hull he found that Peter had joined Mosley and he soon did the same, but none of us were aware that brother Alf from Bolton, who was to become District Leader, had also donned the same shirt.

So there we were, four brothers who without any prior mutual discussion were now all members of this new dynamic Movement! I think the Charnley brothers were unique in this respect. When Bill Leaper, the then editor of The Fascist Week learned of this, our group photograph was published in the paper.

It was therefore with a sense of relief that I heard Peter's proposal that I move in with him in Hull. He was in congenial lodgings, and he knew that his landlady would not be averse to another member of the same family. The move was also pleasing to me because there was already a flourishing branch of the movement in Hull and I knew that I would be immediately catapulted into a new circle of comrades. So I packed my few belongings, said my goodbyes to my many-times landlady in Scarisbrick Street, who was to be a very practical friend in years to come, bade a tearful farewell to Auntie Lizzie, then drove off on my motor bike.

It was to be nearly nine years before I again took up residence in Southport, and there are only a few of those erstwhile Blackshirts that I remember today, and none that I see. Among those that I recollect are Eddie Bowles, who owned a small private hotel near the promenade, Tom Gallon, head chef at the Palace Hotel Birkdale; and Eddie Ayling, whose father had financial interests in Southport Pleasureland.

I met him once shortly before the end of the war in the lounge bar of the Queens Hotel on the promenade. He was in R.A.F. uniform and in the company of other service officers, and although we chatted briefly I discreetly refrained from any reference to our pre-war association. I never saw or heard of him again. Mick Carter was also employed as a commie chef at the Palace Hotel. An Irishman from Dublin, he had been in the armed forces during the war and had been dug out of bombed wreckage in London and invalided out. His spine was severely damaged, but despite this he returned to his trade and became head chef at the Scarisbrick Hotel.

I still see him very occasionally; the last time at Church, but our first meeting after the war was quite exceptional. It was the occasion of my daughter's twenty-first birthday party at the Scarisbrick Hotel, and he requested permission to speak to discover if I was the John Charnley he had known in pre-war Southport.

There were also the two Ashworth brothers from Belfast, the older of the two vehemently anti-Sinn Fein, and yet surprisingly the closest of Blackshirt companions with Mick Carter. They had fought on opposite sides in Ireland but Mosley bonded them together in common endeavour. An impossible achievement in Northern Ireland today, yet in many a B.U.F. branch, Southern Irish Catholics and Northern Protestant worked together amicably.

I met my one-time friend Noni McCarthy on a number of occasions. For a time after the war, during which in the later years he had been in the Army, he and his wife were host and hostess in a local night club. Later when it closed, he worked as a representative for a firm of wine merchants. Jim Highton volunteered for the army in late 1934. I met him after my retirement from my own business and found him as proprietor of a small pet shop in Churchtown, but shortly after he sold the business and moved away. The only other Southport member who I have seen in recent years was a Mr. Harris, a wonderful pianist and professional piano teacher. He was always a very quiet retiring type and it surprised me to find him in Walton Gaol under detention. There I would see him taking a walk, always on his own, a very solitary man. He would gravely acknowledge me but never wanted to enter into conversation. It is a number of years since I saw him, and he has probably died.

So ended another chapter in my life. Southport was again behind me and I was heading towards a new life. As I drove towards Leeds I was tempted to break my journey, but decided it might be unwise to seek out my childhood haunts. I was anxious to get to Hull before dark and rejoin my brother Peter.

I arrived at my new home soon after he had finished work for the day. Peter's landlady was a friendly soul — an elderly widow with two married sons, and in receipt of a pension from Trinity House in addition to her state Widow's Benefit. She was familiarly known as 'Mam Bradley', and was quite a good cook. It was understood that so long as I remained unemployed I would pay a reduced figure for my board and lodging, but I naturally hoped that this would not be for long.

We brothers made no secret of our membership of Mosley's Movement, and no opposition was ever shown to our political views. Within a few weeks of my arrival in Hull, Sydney wrote from Southampton to say that he would shortly be joining us. In the meantime I found a job with a small business operated by two elderly spinster sisters, but regretfully it did not last long. The quality of my work was too professional for them. They wanted their products to be obviously carrying the 'home-made' stamp and for years I had striven for professionalism in my work. It was a new experience to lose a job because my work was too good.

It soon became clear that looking after three men was too much for Mam Bradley, so Syd and I agreed to find alternative accommodation, while Peter would remain.

We had, by now, of course, visited the local headquarters of the Movement, and I was not impressed with either the premises or the administrative official.

I did not have a high opinion of the capabilities of the new Branch Officer. I had been accustomed to the efficiency of Harry Jones, who educationally was clearly OTC type. I was not alone in my condemnatory viewpoint. It was also held by a Captain Fryer, an experienced seaman with his Masters' Ticket, beached because of the general slump in shipping. I think he must have reported on the situation to London because he was appointed Branch Officer, told to close the existing rambling premises, and find a small office with a good address from which he could introduce a new administration. This he did, renting a one-room office in a prestigious building in the city centre, Paragon Buildings, Paragon Square. He provided his own typewriter and arranged for the installation of the telephone. I was quite happy with the new set-up, and knew that under him we would make progress.

By now Syd and I had found suitable living quarters, reasonably near to the city centre and similar to what we had in Southport. One large lounge, a small bedroom enough for two single beds and a composite wardrobe, and the use of a kitchen. We stayed at 58 Albany Street for about a year.

Once again I succeeded in finding work, this time at the co-operative bakery. I was not happy here, however. It was a substantial bakery with a large staff, about forty, and to a man they were the laziest set of workmen it has ever been my misfortune to work with. The deliberate wastage was criminal. I used to be told that I worked too hard and was spoiling the job. It had always been my practise throughout my working life to give an honest day's work for an honest day's pay, and I just could not deliberately and consciously defraud my employers. To me that was stealing.

For the first time I also began to feel the suggestions of political bias, but had not appreciated until then how prevalent the practise was to squeeze as much out of the employer for the least possible expenditure of individual effort. Is that why the productivity of the British workman is consistently well below that of the American and the German, even when, as in the car industry, identical machinery is being used over the same number of man-hours? As a nation, are we downright lazy? I sometimes think we must be.

I was surprised to be told after six weeks that I was unsatisfactory, and that I would have to leave. When I asked the bakery manager in what way was I unsatisfactory he could not tell me. When I asked if it was because I worked too hard he simply glared at me and told me to leave his office. I was happy to oblige.

I soon found another job, this time with W.M. Jackson and Sons Ltd the largest privately-owned bakery in Yorkshire, with shops in a number of towns. They also did a large wholesale trade delivering as far afield as Manchester. The quality of their products was very good, and I remained with them for about two years, the circumstances of my leaving unusual. I was still a member of the Bakers Union, and there was an agreement with most of the larger concerns that they would pay the rate to union members in their employ. There was also an agreement that they would continue to maintain customary conditions, including holidays with pay, which at the time were not obligatory, and paid only at the discretion of the firm. This agreement was also upheld until the Christmas of 1936.

It had been customary to make an ex-gratia payment of eight hours pay for Boxing Day. Most firms paid for Christmas Day, but Boxing Day was additional, though paid for many, many years. Wages were paid weekly on Friday, the night staff receiving their wages before going home in the morning. On the Friday following Christmas Day the night staff collected their wages only to realise that they were not in receipt of the eight hours for Boxing Day. They had been told by the wages clerk that this year, on instructions from the managing director, it was not being paid, a clear breach of a customary practice since no prior notice had been issued. Eight hours pay amounted to a serious drop in expected income in 1936, and there was much expressed dissatisfaction.

It was agreed that where possible, without endangering production and oven attention, we would down tools and request a meeting with the manager. The manager, Mr. Dodsworth, agreed. We all crowded into the canteen but without a spokesman. I was already well known as a local Blackshirt platform speaker and was asked to present our grievance. The result was that he sanctioned the additional payment. He was not, however, pleased with the outcome of our joint action and four weeks later he told me that under a re-organisation my services were to be dispensed with.

So out I went, with a week's wages in lieu of notice. I should have had a claim for wrongful dismissal because under the so-called re-organisation no other operative lost their job. No union action was taken on my behalf, nor did any of my fellow operatives make any protest against my dismissal. I must concede however that unions were not as strong as they were later to become, and there was still much unemployment.

In early 1934 Lord Rothermere gave temporary support to Mosley, beginning with an article in The Daily Mail entitled 'Hurrah for the Blackshirts'. This heralded a period of support in his newspapers which lasted a few months, and was responsible for a sudden influx of members into the branch in Southport, a pattern which was repeated throughout the country.

I have often been asked by interested parties, including television journalists if this support was beneficial in the long term. It would be untruthful not to admit that when the Daily Mail support ceased recruitment did for a time fall. In my own experience I found that Rothermere's support brought in a Kaleidoscope of members, the true value of which could not be assessed at the time. Some of these recruits were milk and water, who could not stand the pace, and fell away when the going became tough. Some were clearly of doubtful character, looking for easy pickings in a mushroom growth which might provide opportunities for exploitation job-wise. Many however were genuine proselytes who became reliable members, though in my experience the majority of those who remained were non-active, and did little to advance our cause.

It was also in 1934 that the first big London indoor meetings were held. I attended all of them from 1934 to 1940, the first at the Royal Albert Hall in April. I had seen the building on previous occasions but only from the outside and had gone down from Southport with a contingent from Lancashire, joined by a large contingent from the Liverpool branch.

It was a wonderful experience not only to absorb the atmosphere of the building but to be aware of what could be history in the making. To appreciate the power and force of Mosley rhetoric you had to be there to hear and to see, and unless you were already a determined and dedicated opponent you just could not fail to be carried away by his sheer magnetism.

What a tragedy that his unmatched talents were lost to the nation, and we were fobbed off with Churchill. If the British people had followed Mosley's lead we could have avoided war. Millions of lives would have been saved, and the subsequent horror of the Holocaust would have been averted.

This Albert Hall meeting was followed two months later by an even larger one at Olympia. So much has already been written about this meeting, most of it fabrication, that I will only write of my own experience.

I could never follow the logic of Mosley's opponents when writing or talking of this meeting in suggesting that he covered the cost of the hire of the hall, the obligatory insurance charges, the advertising, the cost of transporting stewards from varying parts of the country, and selling tickets to the general public, in order to fight the audience and throw them out.

The whole purpose and object of the meeting was to explain his policy to a large audience. We certainly threw out those communist and socialists who attempted to disrupt the meeting, and under provocation, with a great deal of force.

Celebration Dinner at Metropole, Hull on 22nd December, 1936, when Mosley, seated with British Union Director General Neil Francis-Hawkins and other national officers, announced the author as the prospective Parliamentary Candidate for Hull East. The author, behind Mosley, is flanked by Jean Forster, Leader of Hull's women Blackshirts, and her brother Sydney.

After Olympia Mosley's supporters were referred to as thugs. I was typical of the majority of members. There were some, who like Tommy Moran, were well-built and powerful but I, 5' 7", was about nine stone in weight, and slim built. Some thug! What liars Mosley's Marxist and 'Old Gang' opponents were — and still are.

It was at Olympia that I first encountered the B.U.F.'s Director-General, Neil Francis-Hawkins. I was on duty on the balcony which surrounded the main body of the hall. A member of the Red Front had climbed one of the main roof girders and was causing a disturbance. Without pausing to consider the wisdom of my action I started to climb up after him, but Francis-Hawkins who was just behind me pulled me down. After telling me not to be a fool, he climbed the girder, and eventually persuaded the interrupter to come down. What surprised me most at the meeting was the patience shown by the bulk of the 12,500 audience until order was restored, and the warm reception which they accorded Mosley at the conclusion of his address.

Neil Francis-Hawkins was in many ways a complete opposite of the swashbuckling Elizabethan sea captain of the same name from whom he was descended. Never a public speaker or exponent of written propaganda, he ran the administration of National Headquarters and the movement generally with calm order and meticulous efficiency. He was completely loyal to Mosley from the day, in 1932, when he led the majority of the old British Fascists into British Union until his untimely death in 1950 at the age of 47, and Mosley, in return, put his complete trust in his abilities. Colleagues found him very much a private man, always accessible but difficult to get close to. Perhaps this was exactly what was needed in a man who had to exercise some control over the diverse band of spirited men and women who formed the backbone of British Union.

His devotion to duty was legendary within the movement and he had considerable courage as was shown in his handling of the Olympia incident already mentioned. His honesty in all matters was beyond question, which even the 18b Advisory Committee was forced to admit. Sadly he suffered greatly from lengthy wartime confinement in Brixton Jail and from left-wing harassment after the war when, penniless, he tried to find employment. Mosley was convinced that this vindictive imprisonment of a man suffering from chronic bronchial asthma brought his early death. Of one thing I am sure, British Union could never have had a better Director General.

In September, of that same year, the first of the big London propaganda marches was held culminating in a massed rally in Hyde Park. It was a long march and when we arrived in our allotted area in Hyde Park I was feeling somewhat drained. For the first time I saw Eric Hamilton Piercy in the flesh. I had seen his photograph in our weekly paper on a number of occasions, and I was impressed with his smart appearance.

Mosley and Eric Hamilton Piercy with the famous "I Squad", Hyde Park, 1934.

For some time he had been in charge of the famous "I Squad" a special defence force for major meetings, and it was considered a mark of honour to be elected to the elite body. He ceased full-time participation in the Movement at the time of financial retrenchment in 1936, but was detained under Regulation 18b.

He and his friend and BU member C.P.P. Dick had run a nonstop ferry service throughout the Dunkirk evacuation in Dick's forty foot open bridged motor launch 'Advance', bringing back large numbers of British soldiers to our shores. An official report stated that Dick and Piercy, then 39, had volunteered to take themselves to Sheerness after hearing there was an acute shortage of crews for the evacuation. By persistence they took 'Advance' to Sheerness and then Dunkirk.

What the report did not reveal was that they were arrested on their final return and taken to Walton Gaol. This was the type of men whose incarceration was sanctioned by Churchill[1].

I recall some of the other fine men and women who played prominent parts in our national movement. Bill Risdon, for example, an industrial specialist and former member of the Independent Labour Party, was the British Union election organiser.

A retiring personality, very likable, he was a competent speaker who gave a cool, logical exposition of economic policy. A.K. Chesterton, another prominent figure, I never met. But John Beckett, the former Labour MP who attracted national prominence when he lifted the Speaker's Mace from its place in the House of Commons in protest against Government policy, was an excellent speaker in our cause. Like his friend, William Joyce, he loved to antagonise a section of his audience. Some speakers are like that. He was knowledgeable, and a character, but I wasn't sorry to see him go in March 1937, following a reorganisation at National Headquarters. I felt there was something about his character that I didn't altogether like, though I could never put my finger on it.

Mick Clarke of East London ... now there was a charismatic individual! In my opinion he was the only British Union speaker who had anything approaching the platform charisma of Mosley. He had his own style, not O.M's at all, but he possessed this ability to take hold of an audience and ring it until their very withers withered away. A genuine Cockney, he was an outstanding street corner tub-thumper, with a tremendous following in East London, where he was known as "The Idol of Bethnal Green".

I have recalled William Joyce's platform appearance at Liverpool Stadium in November 1933. What a vitriolic tongue! But personality? You could almost feel the vibrations of his personality coming over the loudspeakers. Like Beckett, he would do

1   Comrade, June/July 1988.

Mick Clarke: British Union speaker who attracted large crowds in
London's East End.

nothing to placate an audience. He was also openly anti-Jewish.
Anti-Semitism didn't necessarily bring British Union long-
lasting members. They joined the movement on a fringe whim,
and rarely felt at home with the main philosophy and policies of
the Movement. William Joyce tended to encourage this type of
recruit, who we would have been better off without.

But I must say, in the light of what followed, that when I talked
to his brother, Frank, during my period of Internment at Ascot
Camp, he assured me that when Joyce left Britain for Germany
he had no intention or desire to damage his country. According
to Frank, he went there convinced that within a very short space
of time, the anti-war forces would be silenced, and that by going
to Germany he would be able to bring about a negotiated peace.

There was another reason for William Joyce's departure which I
had no idea about at the time. Evidently he had contacts in MI5

that went back to before the days of British Union. When he was Mosley's Director of Propaganda MI5 had asked Joyce to go to Germany, work his way into National Socialist circles there and send back inside information. Not surprisingly he declined. Just before the outbreak of war, one of Joyce's MI5 contacts phoned him late one night. The officer told him his name was on the first list of people to be detained under Regulation 18b which was to be implemented in forty-eight hours time[2].

The thought of spending the war sitting helplessly in some cell, while outside history was being decided without him, would have been anathema to Joyce. So without waiting further, he slipped across to the continent while he still had the chance.

At the end of the war, I actually wrote to William Joyce when he was in prison, awaiting trial. I cannot recall exactly what I said, but I remember expressing personal regret over his present circumstances, and recalling with gladness the days when I had known him in British Union. I did not get, nor did I expect to receive, a reply. There was an inherent honesty about the man, a refusal to countenance dishonesty in any way or in any person, whether in political or general behaviour. I liked him very much.

Alexander Raven Thomson, a fighter-intellectual, breathed political and philosophical truth. A very good platform speaker, he deputised for Mosley in Hull on one occasion, when we had a wonderful meeting. Whereas Becket produced a noisy, rowdy meeting, Raven, as we called him in the movement, created a feeling of something approaching euphoria among his audience. He had a style entirely of his own, disarming his opponents before they were able to utter anything in opposition.

Before joining British Union, Raven had written a book 'Civilisation as Divine Superman' (1932), which established his credentials as a student of philosophy. What the rank and file admired about him most was that unlike the majority of intel-

---

2   Truth Betrayed, W.J. West 1987

lectuals he had the courage to come out of the study and fight for his ideas on the streets of Britain, and stay the course despite all the danger that this brought. He was, indeed, a fine example of what Mosley called the Warrior-Poet, or Thought-Deed Man: somebody who could both think and act.

Alexander Raven Thompson, BUF Director of Policy was to suffer mental and physical torture whilst under detention.

After his conversion from communism he rose rapidly through the ranks of the Blackshirt Movement and his remarkable gifts as a creative intellectual were soon rewarded with the title of Director of Policy. It was Raven who wrote 'The Coming Corporate State' in which he spelt out in precise detail a workable plan for the regeneration of British industry that combined progress with economic justice. He suffered severely during wartime imprisonment being subject to the mental and physical torture methods meted out at the notorious Latchmere House interrogation centre at Ham Common, Richmond. His anguish during this period was increased by the death of his son on active service with the RAF. Raven's wife was German and the son had asked his father during the war what he should do. Raven never hesitated in his answer: "Fight to defend Britain".

Raven's commitment to Mosley never wavered either: after the war he became Secretary of Union Movement and he embraced the new creed of Europe A Nation while developing his own syndicalist ideals of Worker Ownership which became Union Movement policy. The strain of his wartime treatment eventually began to take its toll and Raven suffered first a heart attack and the following year developed incurable cancer. While dying in St. George's Hospital, Hyde Park Corner, he still found the will and the strength to drag himself out of bed to attend one final important Union Movement conference. With a dozen more like Raven it might have been a different story: a wonderful man, immensely popular, he served the Movement until the last moment before his early death in 1955.

In 1936 our campaign 'Stand by The King' was launched in a vain attempt to arrest the move towards Edward VIII's removal from the throne. His popularity could not be gainsaid and a morganatic marriage could, if carefully handled, have been found acceptable to the country. I was surprised at the speech at which his removal was effected. I had anticipated a much longer campaign, and disappointed that he had not made a greater effort to remain on the Throne.

The Constitution at the time would have permitted him to dismiss Parliament, appoint Ministers of his own choosing and rule by Royal Decree through those Ministers for a maximum period of either three or five years had he done so. Had he done so, Mosley might have been one of his chosen Ministers. Shortly after the abdication the Constitution was altered so that a similar situation could not arise again.

Early the following year I was discussing the Abdication with Mosley, expressing my regrets at what I considered our lost opportunity. I clearly remember his closing comment: "He had no enthusiasm for the job and in any case you cannot continue fighting for a man who will not fight for himself. When an opportunity is irretrievably lost do not waste time in useless regret".

Early in 1936 Captain Fryer obtained a good position as Harbour Master in the Port of Bahrain. By now I had become a fairly good speaker and was holding regular meetings at the various recognised open-air sites in Hull. I was working closely with Captain Fryer to re-create a sound branch of the movement in the town and he had appointed me, with N.H.Q. approval, his Propaganda Officer.

When he learned of his appointment, he recommended that I be appointed Branch Officer, or District Leader as we were now designated, and Francis-Hawkins approved my promotion. In addition I was also made Propaganda Officer for East Yorkshire. Although I was flattered by the appointment it meant that I would have to extend the area of my activities.

There were now a number of salaried speakers on the B.U.F.'s staff, as well as Area Inspectors. Of the staff speakers I knew Tommy Moran, Aleck Miles and Alex Broad. It was possible on request to arrange for a staff speaker to be allocated to your area for a limited period, and through this method I used the services of all three.

I would advertise meetings by use of whitewash and brush, but this was not always an advantage since it allowed the opposition to organise counter-demonstrations which often resulted in street fights. I never was bruiser material, and would avoid actual conflict if I could do so without loss of face. I have stood and fought on many occasions when I would have preferred to withdraw.

Alex Broad was an ex-R.A.F. man who invariably wore his wings on his uniform black shirt. He was a good speaker too, with a stringent wit, whereas I was always too serious in my style of delivery. Tommy, of course, could always pull a crowd, and one never need be afraid of a fight if Tommy was at your side, and to a slightly lesser extent the same could be said of Alex Broad. But not Aleck Miles. He was too much of the professional speaker type. I later discovered that this was exactly what he was. He knew the policy but his delivery did not have the ring of sincerity and truth. He had earlier been in the employ of The Economic League, a quasi political-economic conglomerate financed by industry, perhaps even by the National Council of Trade, to which organisation I was to devote so much of my time in my post-war business years. I was once asked by Hector McKecknie, who was in charge of national meetings and was responsible for staff speakers, to report on Aleck Miles, and he was later dismissed. He was soon on another platform, however, speaking for a titled lady campaigning for the abolition of capital punishment, as well as supporting Beaverbrook's "Empire Crusade". I too was offered the chance of mounting the same platform for a salary far in excess of my earnings, but was too committed to Mosley to even consider it.

In 1936 a programme of weekend speakers' schools was introduced to improve the quality of existing and budding new speakers. These were held regularly at the Leeds headquarters, and I often attended. It was here that I first met William Joyce on a personal level, also many other senior officials such as John Sant, John Hone, Captain B.D.E. Donovan, Hector McKecknie, Lieutenant Colonel Sharpe and Peter Whittam, National Inspector for the North East. Peter was also quite a good speaker, although easily rattled by a noisy crowd. He was a good man to have with you, though, in an emergency full of guts and enthusiasm.

I had tried, through McKecknie, to secure a Leader's Meeting in Hull but with no success to date. I got John Beckett for a medium-sized hall, and the meeting started off rather rowdy. It was held in the Fulford Rooms on Beverly Road, and was the first time that I met Dick Bellamy, National Inspector, working from offices in Corporation Street, Manchester. Due to continued interruptions and the clamour of constant scuffles an elderly lady wanted to leave. I was in charge of the exits on to the main road. Dick escorted the lady to the rear of the hall and asked me to open the door. I knew we had a very rowdy crowd outside and I expected trouble. When I opened it we were met with a hail of bricks, and Bellamy was so incensed that he dashed across the wide footpath waving his arms and shouting "Oh you swine, you despicable swine!". The police were in evidence and assisted the elderly lady away from the entrance, but Dick and I were involved in more fighting before we were able to return to the hall. From that moment he was someone special in my life. Only one other man has made a greater impression on me and it was especially important that I joined with Dick a few years ago to talk of our association with Oswald Mosley in the BBC television documentary "Britain in the Thirties".

As a youth Dick had led an adventurous life as a 'jackaroo' in the Australian outback and a coffee planter working among cannibals in New Caledonia. He told of these exciting times in two books: 'The Real South Seas' and 'Mixed Bliss in Melanesia'. Dick was a superb story-teller and the latter book was described by the OBSERVER as "The best travel book of the year". He returned to this country in the early 1930s and was shocked by the poverty and conditions he found. Within a few months of its foundation, Dick joined British Union and eventually became Senior Staff Officer in charge of Northern Headquarters based in Manchester. He was selected as our parliamentary candidate for Blackley in readiness for the General Election of 1940 that never came. Dick described his period as National Inspector for the region as "probably the happiest time of my life"[3]

It was eventually agreed that we were to have a Mosley meeting in Hull. The local authority refused us the use of the Guild Hall and the management of the Astoria Cinema pulled out of a verbal agreement following threats of violence and possible damage to the cinema. The only alternative was an open-air meeting. I have been at Olympia, Holbeck Moor, Leeds, and Royal Mint Street, London, all of which were rough, but none was so rough and tough throughout the whole of my seven years in the prewar movement than at Corporation Field, Hull, in July 1936.

The trouble which developed, and the size of the opposition that had assembled there before our arrival, was absolutely

---

3   Shortly after the War Richard Reynall Bellamy became British Union's official historian, authorised by Mosley to "write our story" before it was forgotten and lost. Bellamy spent the next 30 years completing a magnum opus of over 300,000 words which has recently been edited into the yet unpublished We Marched with Mosley, Mosley in Perspective, and Memoirs of a Fascist Beast. He died in 1988 in his 88th year. His friend, the author, survived him by 4 months.

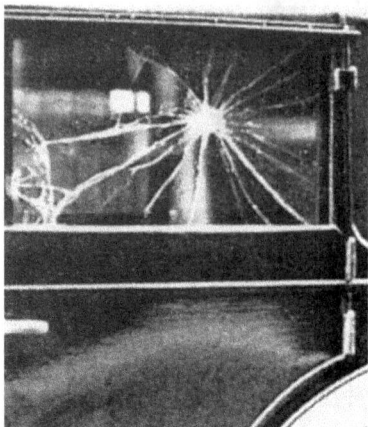

beyond my comprehension. It was obvious before the meeting started that there was going to be very serious trouble. But the opposition was so vicious that it is difficult to make people who weren't there understand and appreciate the reality.

At this meeting every type of weapon was used, and the fight went on for over an hour. It was alleged that an attempt had been made on O.M.'s life, and a bullet hole was certainly found in the windscreen of his car.

At the height of the battle, Yorkshire National Inspector, Peter Whittam yelled out at the top of his voice, "This can't go on. Get your bloody belts off!" We did, and using them in self-defence, kept our frenzied assailants at bay.

The press later alleged that we had attacked the crowd with steel-buckled belts. We did not attack the crowd. I was in charge of that meeting. I wanted new members, and to get them I had organised that meeting so that the audience could listen to Mosley explaining our policy. How I wish I could dispel the lies that were so often told about us!

The Chief Constable eventually arrived at the meeting, and advised Mosley, Francis-Hawkins as the administrative organiser, and myself as the local organiser, to call the meeting off otherwise he would use his powers to read "The Riot Act". Mosley got down from the coal cart which we had been using as a platform and asked me to arrange for a departure from the field.

The crowd was still very hostile, and I had to try to arrange an orderly withdrawal. We formed up into a column three abreast ready to move off. It fell to me to lead it since I was in charge and had to take the visiting stewards back to the garage where their coaches were stationed.

We were completely surrounded by a howling mob literally screaming for our blood, and I was frightened. If I said otherwise I would be a liar. I was scared, and Mosley knew it. He tapped me on the shoulder and said, "Which direction do we have to go?" And I pointed the way. "Right", he said, "Start marching in that direction and I promise you, that provided you show no fear, that crowd will open up and let us through. I know that you can do it, and don't forget that I am right behind you". He looked at me, nodded his head and said "Now", and I moved.

How I did it I don't know, there were a few scuffles, and once we had to stop to re-form. We got off that field carrying our wounded and marched back to our headquarters, half a mile away. We had over twenty hospital cases for the outpatients department, but fortunately no one was kept in. The Reds, however, had over a hundred. We had given a good account of ourselves!

When we left the field the police collected the opposition's weapons from the battle ground. They included brush staves with six-inch nails in the end, bicycle chains, lengths of ship's steel hawser, knuckledusters, raw potatoes studded with razor blades and thick woollen stockings with broken glass in the heel and foot.

Subsequent official reports completely exonerated the Blackshirts, placing the blame fairly and squarely on the Communist opposition. You will read little or nothing of this in the "histories" and "social documentaries" written and broadcast by their supporters and apologists within the media and the British Establishment.

I quote from a report made by Inspector J. Holmes (HO 144/21060 92242/20, folio 154).

"The Fascists were not to blame as nothing was said or done to provoke the crowd. They did not interfere with anyone until bricks and other missiles were thrown, and one of the party seriously injured. Several others received minor injuries."

Another officer, Sgt. T.A. Sawdon reported (folio 160/161)

. . . "owing to the violence of the crowd it was impossible to take anyone into custody for these assaults, as we had our work cut out to protect ourselves. At no time did I see any action on the part of the Blackshirts that was likely to provoke the crowd into the way they acted".

The Blackshirt "seriously injured" had been hit in the face with a half-brick, and when he fell to the ground, received a second brick on the head. Another Blackshirt, B.H. Taylor from Doncaster, suffered "severe head and face injuries", while W.A. Milligan from Sheffield, sustained "serious head and facial injuries. Front teeth split from edge upwards to the roots, inner pulp being damaged. Crushed tooth nerves. Teeth will eventually have to be removed".

In all, 8 of the 21 Blackshirts injured had head wounds, one of them being John Charnley.

I was working at Jacksons at this time and the next day I was on 6 a.m. start. There were many strange looks but no condemnatory remarks. One man said, "You must have a lot of guts", and that pleased me. I finished my shift at two o'clock, and whether out of bravado or because I was stupid I carried my speaker's stand down to the Labour Exchange and held a short meeting. I met with no opposition, probably because my action was not expected.

Shortly before the meeting, on the Corporation Field, my two brothers and I discussed the idea of renting suitable property which we could use not only as a home but also as suitable headquarters. We would jointly become the tenants and the office rent now being paid for headquarters could be transferred as a contributory rent income. I discussed the idea with Francis-Hawkins and he was agreeable. We soon found a suitable property on Spring Bank not far where Syd and I were now living.

It was a large three-storey building, with extensive room space on the ground floor and an abundance of living space above. The ground floor was utilised as office, club rooms and kitchen. It was a good site and a good address and the property was in fine condition. We had a dormitory on the top floor where we often accommodated visiting officials for overnight stops. Shortly after moving in, two brothers, both of whom were members, also joined us as tenants.

So the three brothers were together again living under the same roof. Peter had now left Melias and joined a local firm — the one that I also worked for — he on the grocery side of the business, me in the bakery. A long-standing friend of Peter used to come in twice weekly to see to the cleaning and laundry, and on these days would also cook a hot meal for us. Later she was to become a good friend to my wife.

We settled into a routine. Unless we were acting as stewards for a Leader's meeting in another town, Sunday was always free of local politics. Monday evening was always devoted to a member's meeting in a large room used for this purpose, when the programme of the week would be discussed and agreed. I had a very good treasurer in Jim Bellini, whose accounting was always detailed and up-to-date. It was his responsibility to collect subscriptions from active members, and to arrange his own system of collecting subscriptions from non-active members, who seldom attended headquarters. He was also responsible for the ordering and distribution of our weekly paper for street sales, and delivery to regular readers. He was a member of the army reserve, and I sorely missed him when he was recalled to his regiment shortly after Chamberlain's Guarantee to Poland.

The duties of treasurer were then taken up by one of the lodger brothers, Vic King. Although not arrested at the same time he was later to join me in Walton Gaol. He still lives in Yorkshire and we correspond, but infrequently.

National Headquarters produced a wide selection of pamphlets dealing with the many different aspects of our policy. Mosley was the only politician, up to present, who had a detailed policy for every section of trade, industry and commerce. There was not a single problem of national life that he had not analysed and evaluated. In this he was and will remain unique.

These policy leaflets were available at a nominal charge, and we would carry out house-to-house distribution, including back copies of our paper to stimulate interest in our policies.

Thursday evenings, weather permitting, would be devoted to a street meeting. Hull had many sites for permitted open-air meetings, my favourite site being Baker Street, a side street of Prospect Street and close to the city centre.

In the summer months we would often cycle out to either Beverly or Diffield, both small agricultural towns, and on rare occasions would even go as far afield as Market Weighton, but for this we had to lay on motor transport.

I could no longer afford to run a motor-bike and had sold mine shortly after arriving in Hull. Twice we even travelled across the Humber to hold meetings in Grimsby, but we discontinued them because it necessitated a race back to New Holland to catch the last ferry to Hull. Saturday nights were devoted exclusively to street sales. We would have anything from six to a dozen members on selected sites from 7.30 to 9.30, just enough time left for a quick drink before the pubs closed!

The Communist Party influence in Hull was greater than anywhere outside London, with the possible exception of Glasgow, and it very often made itself evident at our open-air meetings. As for ourselves, we attracted the widest possible range of people into the Hull branch of British Union. A very large proportion were working class, many — like our Communist opponents — connected with the docks.

There were also small businessmen, a couple of solicitors, even a barrister, two dentists, two or three doctors — the widest spectrum of the community. Throughout its life, British Union drew its support and active membership from every strata of society. Mosley attracted people towards him like a magnet, and it didn't matter what section of life you came from.

The old saying, "Once with us, Always with us" proved to be very true in my long experience. I have never come across anyone who, once having declared their loyalty to Mosley, ever became violently anti-Mosley. Quite a number were apathetic, particularly during the war years and after, but overall, once with Mosley, always with Mosley.

In the autumn we took time off from local activities to take part in the BUF's Fourth Anniversary demonstration which was to take place in East London which was to become the media's 'Battle of Cable Street'. Several thousand Blackshirts were to march from the Royal Mint to Limehouse, Shoreditch, Bow and Bethnal Green in each of which Mosley would speak.

For weeks the Communists had agitated to prevent it taking place and on the day, October 4th, they erected barricades in Cable Street and other nearby streets, and fierce battles developed with the police who went in to clear them. To prevent further disorder, the Police Commissioner, Sir Philip Game, after securing the Home Secretary's approval, ordered the march to be called off, and Mosley, lined up with his Blackshirts half-a-mile away, and whose maxim was 'uphold the law until we change it', marched with his thousands in the opposite direction to be finally dismissed on the Thames Embankment at Westminster.

The mass of Mosley's men had not been involved in the fighting except for a small number who were early arrivals at the meeting place where they were met by hundreds of Reds armed with a variety of weapons, and we were to arrive in the thick of it.

Peter Whittam and I had travelled down overnight with Blackshirts from Hull and Leeds in our Bedford trucks we named our 'agony wagons', and on arrival the street fight was at its height and I saw my old friend Tommy Moran go down from a blow to the head from what looked like a pickaxe handle — as it turned out to be, covered in barbed wire. He appeared to be badly injured with blood pouring from a gash high on the forehead and across the scalp. To my amazement within minutes I saw him rise from the ground, blood seeping from a roughly bandaged head, and re-enter the fray putting many of his opponents to the ground. We won that scrimmage and made our way to our assembly point. It always surprises me that in the heat of battle one seldom experiences fear, and the example and sheer guts of Tommy on that occasion never loses its clarity. He was a great fighter and a source of constant inspiration.

After dismissal on the Embankment many Blackshirts made their way to the BUF National Headquarters in Gt. Smith Street where Mosley from an upstairs window spoke to them in words never to be forgotten.

"We never surrender" he said. "We shall triumph over the parties of corruption because our faith is greater than their faith, our will is stronger than their will, and within us the flame that shall light this country and shall later light the world."

The Communists and their left-wing allies portrayed it as 'great rising of East London workers against Mosley' but the truth was that the mobs had been gathered from all over Britain and this proved to be the catalyst which created massive support for Mosley and British Union in traditionally patriotic working class East London.

Two weeks later Mosley addressed cheering thousands at several massive street meetings in East London. Called at a few hours notice there was not a sign of those that 'stopped' Mosley at Cable Street and six months later Blackshirt candidates polled nearly 20 per cent of the votes in the LCC elections in those boroughs through which he had been prevented from marching on October 4th.

As a consequence of the Communist organised street disorder, Parliament passed the Public Order Act making it illegal after the end of 1936 to wear political uniforms in public which left me feeling very incensed. It was a political act, pure and simple, directed exclusively against our Movement in the hope of putting a break on its appeal.

I was most pleased to wear my uniform for the last time on a very special personal occasion. The BUF had not contested seats in the 1935 General Election but decided to choose candidates for the next, which could not be expected before 1940, and much to my surprise I was asked to stand in the Hull East Constituency. We already had a sub-branch there under the leadership of Frank Danby, a devoted and indefatigable worker and I agreed to be adopted, and we had a celebration on December 22nd at the Metropole, a large meeting room.

Mosley and Director General Francis-Hawkins attended as guests and it was a very proud moment when Oswald Mosley made the after dinner announcement. I don't remember much of my reply except the closing words. "When Mosley leads, what is there for me to do but follow?" I am still following him and shall continue to do so until the end of my life.

In his speech Mosley also referred to the meeting at Corporation Fields saying "Always we come back and always we win, and always in the end we achieve our objectives. . . as in the end the Blackshirt Movement will achieve power and save this country".

And back he came in June to Corporation Fields, almost a year after our 1936 battle, and spoke to a police estimated crowd of 10,000. A small bunch of Reds were no more than a nuisance value and Mosley led a march from District Headquarters and back again afterwards. He promised he would be back. He always kept his promise.

As I have said, 1937 brought the banning of the Blackshirt uniform which at the time I had considered to be essential to our continued progress, and I pondered on ways whereby we might legally overcome it. I felt that the uniform helped to sell our weekly paper as it made us distinctive and stimulated attention.

We used to have armbands on the sleeve of the uniform and I assumed that we might get away with wearing them on civilian clothing. A number of us wore them for our usual Baker Street meetings, but at the conclusion of one the police sergeant in attendance warned me that if we wore them again he might be instructed to charge us with breaking the law.

I thought, or rather hoped, that this was only a threat without any follow-up. We adopted the same tactic the following week and on this occasion I was allowed to finish the meeting only to be arrested and taken to the Central Police Station in Alfred Gelder Street. There I was charged with contravening the Public Order Act, but allowed to leave having been told by another sergeant of police that I would have to answer to a summons.

The summons duly came, and I had to appear before the local Stipendiary Magistrate, Mr. MacDonald. I was defended by a counsel provided by London, and during the process of the hearing I was asked for comments in my own defence.

I asked permission to ask the Stipendiary a question, and my question was: "If a number of men wearing striped trousers and bowler hats and carrying umbrellas attended a Conservative Party meeting, would it be considered that they were wearing a political uniform?" This was in answer to the preamble during which the magistrate had said that we were similarly dressed, in that we were all wearing armbands carrying the motif of a political party. As of course we were. The armband carried the symbol of British Union, which was The Flash and Circle.

The magistrate told me not to be insolent to the court. In his summation he said that as the badge on the armband was the accepted symbol of a political party, the wearing of that badge by more than one person at a political gathering constituted, in his opinion, uniformity of dress and as such could be lawfully construed as constituting a breach of Parliamentary Legislation.

I was found guilty and fined ten pounds, then equal to one month's wages. Parliament was guilty of deliberate subterfuge. As MacDonald said, "Parliament did not define a political uniform in its legislation and it had been left to the courts to interpret the law". I became less and less impressed with "Democratic" integrity. The Act had clearly been passed in the vain hope of stunting us.

We settled into a pattern which hardly varied until the emergence of the Munich crisis, which threw us into a spate of activity of meetings and slogan-writing in the Peace Campaign. I held so many peace meetings, many with the slogan of 'No-War for Warsaw', that I went down with a severe bout of bronchitis, and was off work for ten days. My employer did not once complain, although he must have known that it was the strain of the additional meetings which finally took its toll. I held a meeting every night for nearly three weeks until, as we thought, the crisis had passed. We did not realise it was to be repeated the following year.

During the summer and early autumn I had made a number of visits to Southport, always on Sunday unless committed to a Leader's Meeting, sometimes accompanied by Vic King. He was a good driver, and employed as a driver of a railway parcels delivery van. On the last weekend of October I asked my employer for a long weekend, giving me Saturday and Monday and Tuesday off. On the Monday afternoon Edith and I were married, with my brother Alf from Bolton as best man.

Only my brothers and a few close friends knew of my plans. On the Tuesday Edith and I returned to Hull with my four-and-a-half year old daughter, Rose. Alf and his wife Margaret, and Vic King, were the only ones who had met Edith before our wedding day. They had also, of course, met Rose.

At Edith's suggestion we broke our journey at Blackburn to see my father and stepmother. I had told them of my intention to marry and invited them to the wedding but they declined. Nor did we receive a wedding present, though I was scarcely surprised since it was in pattern with previous practise. We were made welcome and my father made quite a fuss of Rose. I was the youngest of his children, but the first to present him with a grandchild, and Rose became a favourite with him.

When we returned to Hull no one expressed surprise that I had suddenly blossomed forth with a wife and daughter. Both were immediately accepted and Rose, a very bonny child with dark brown eyes and black curly hair, became quite a favourite with the members, both male and female. She is now married and also lives in Southport, and is a regular visitor to our house.

A month later Edith had to return to Southport for the funeral of her father. We had known for some time that he was suffering from terminal cancer and I had seen him at his home after our wedding, and had not expected the end to come so quickly. After a short stay with her mother, my wife and daughter returned to Hull. A few weeks later on December 3rd, we received a telegram from my brother in Bolton to say that our stepmother had died unexpectedly. She had contracted a severe chill which developed into pneumonia, and because of an unknown weakness of the heart, did not survive the crisis period. Antibiotics were still in an experimental stage and were, then, not available for general prescription. This news was quite shattering, particularly coming after my wife's loss.

We travelled over to Blackburn on Christmas Day. It was bitterly cold and the train journey was a nightmare with numerous stops and changes. After leaving Hull in the early morning we arrived in the late evening quite exhausted. Rose had been particularly upset and troubled by the whole occasion and I was concerned as to her ability to withstand the strain. I was unpractised as a father and was worrying unnecessarily.

The funeral took place the following day, Boxing Day, with a Requiem Mass at St. Peter's. The church was above the school and access was via a steep stairway with acute turns, and it was customary for the coffin to be brought into the church for the funeral service. Four of the five brothers acted as pall bearers, and I was scared out of my wits lest the coffin fell during the ascent and descent of those nightmare stone stairs. We then had a long drive to a graveyard attached to Pleasington Priory, well on the outskirts of the town. My natural mother was buried in the main Blackburn cemetery and I had only visited her grave on one occasion, shortly after our return to Blackburn from Leeds. I had no memories of her. Can one think with any semblance of affection of a person whom one has not actually known? Back in Hull, life settled into a new pattern, with much of the household responsibility moved from my shoulders and undertaken by my wife.

With the British Government's guarantee to Poland, and the stepping up of an armament's programme, unemployment began to show real signs of ceasing to be a major economic problem. But talk of the possibility of war began to be heard once again as more and more political speeches from the major parties became increasingly belligerent.

British Union was now involved in a Peace Campaign and

demands on me increased as we were pressed to make even greater efforts to avert war. In July 1939 our Campaign culminated in the largest indoor political meeting ever held anywhere in the world, at Earls Court, London.

It was, needless to say, the most spectacular political meeting I ever attended. There had been a rehearsal on the afternoon, Sunday July 16th, but it didn't have any particular impact, since the hall was more or less empty except for a small number of stewards. The whole orchestration of the meeting was in the hands of John Hone, which is not generally realised.

I was positioned in the top gallery, and the atmosphere of the evening, as the time of the meeting approached, was intense. Proceedings opened with a fanfare of trumpets, followed by the pageantry of the British Union Drum Corps leading the massed flags and Honour Standards of hundreds of branches.

It was a huge hall, with a vast audience, most of whom were anti-war even if they were not all pro-Mosley. The people began to stand up and cheer.

The cry "Mosley . . . Mosley . . . Mosley . . . Mosley" echoed down the hall, rising up to the balcony in an ever-increasing crescendo of sound. Then suddenly the whole audience was on its feet. They clapped, they roared, they cheered. And Mosley hadn't even arrived! When the standards stations were taken up at the front of the hall, there was absolute silence. The roll of drums and a searchlight drawn down the centre of the hall, and in the far distance you could see the figure in black.

The uniform had been abolished, but there stood Mosley in a dark suit, black shirt and tie. He marched down the centre aisle unescorted, and as he did so the cheers began to rise, developing and expanding until I thought the roof would come down! This was the man upon whom we had pinned our hopes, the man who could save our country and Empire, and lift our people from

Oswald Mosley addresses 30,000 people Earl's Court
"Britain First" Peace Rally 16th July 1939.

poverty and demoralisation to ever greater heights! He made
his way towards the most unusual plinth upon which he was to
speak, a sort of boom projecting into the auditorium. The people
were shouting and cheering, and just going mad. He raised his
hand, and slowly . . . silence. Then he began. I think it was the
finest speech he ever delivered. At many points he had to stop
speaking because of the wave of applause.

Mosley's great theme was peace, but he also addressed the other
issues which had dominated his 7 year crusade in British Union,
notably the power of international finance.

"We have shown over and over again in infinite detail how the
money and credit of the British people, created by the exertions
of the British people and by no other force on earth, has been
used for their own destruction in the equipment of the Orient
with its sweated labour to undercut and to destroy the West; in

order that usury, international usury, may draw its dividends and its interest by destroying the country of its origin through the equipment of our worldwide competitors against us. We have shown again and again how the British Empire, as well as the British people, the British industrialist and the British worker, has been relentlessly sacrificed to this international power; how the whole of our international trading system, how our conflicting party system, and our foreign policy above all, is maintained for one reason and for one reason alone — that the money power of the world may rule the British people and through them may rule mankind". And then, at the end of some two hours came the final electrifying moments of his peroration.

"I ask the audience, here tonight, whether or not we are going to give everything we have within us, not only material resources but our moral and spiritual being, our very life and our very soul in holy dedication to England that she shall not perish, but shall live in greatness. We are going, if the power lies within us — and it lies within us because within us is the spirit of the English — to say that our generation and our children shall not die like rats in Polish holes. They shall not die but they shall live to breathe the good English air, to love the fair English countryside, to see about them the English sky, to feel beneath their feet the English soil.

This heritage of England, by our struggle and our sacrifice, again we shall give to our children. And with that sacred gift, we tell them that they come from that stock of men who went out from this small island in frail craft across storm-tossed seas to take in their brave hands the greatest Empire that man has ever seen; in which tomorrow our people shall create the highest civilisation that man has ever known. Remember those, who through the centuries have died, that Britain might live in greatness, in beauty and in splendour. Remember too, that in the spiritual values that our creed brings back to earth, these mighty spirits march beside you and you must be worthy of their company.

So we take by the hand these our children to whom our struggle shall give back our England; with them we dedicate ourselves again to the memory of those who have gone before, and to that radiant wonder of finer and noble life that our victory shall bring to our country. To the dead heroes of Britain in sacred union we say — Like you we give ourselves to England: across the ages that divide us — across the glories of Britain that unite us — we gaze into your eyes and we give to you this holy vow: We will be true — today, tomorrow and for ever — England Lives!"

I was certain in my own mind that though we were on the point of war, we had finally broken through the barrier of opposition to our campaign, and that the forces of muddle and evil that were dragging Britain into bitterness and bloodshed would be defeated. We were there! . . . we'd achieved it ... ! we had everything to live for!

People were shouting and cheering, laughing, and, yes . . . crying. I could not believe that after such a mighty demonstration for peace, war could possibly come. It was the greatest demonstration for peace that this country has seen or is ever likely to.

Of course, there were demonstrations at the close of the war, but they were mainly to celebrate victory over an enemy. They were demonstrations of hope and relief from pain, anxiety, fear and death. But those who were with me in that hall at Earls Court on that July evening in 1939 witnessed an incredible demonstration for peace. Never let this be forgotten. We wanted peace and we could have had it, and with honour, and Mosley was the man who could have given it to us.

Destiny and the politicians decided otherwise. Six weeks later the British Government declared war, and within less than a year of that great Earls Court rally, Mosley and hundreds of men and women who had campaigned for an honourable peace, just as they had fought for a better and nobler Britain, had been thrown into prison. Indeed, within days of Earls Court it had become evident that our hopes for peace were premature. Encouraged by the blank cheque assurances of the British Cabinet, the Polish Government became less inclined to take part in discussions with Germany on the future of Danzig and the sovereignty of the Polish Corridor.

Hitler had told Chamberlain at Munich that he had no further territorial ambitions, and Danzig, which was and always had been 95% German, scarcely seemed a logical cause in which to shed the blood of Britons. It should not be forgotten either that Chamberlain had assured Hitler that no dispute between the two Governments would be allowed to develop into war. He had also affirmed that any differences would be discussed around a table in a spirit of friendship. This is conveniently forgotten today. In 1939 I was naive enough to believe that such solemn promises would be kept, and I failed to grasp the dimensions of the gathering storm.

What was significant however, and ultimately decisive, was the implications of the Polish Guarantee. That Britain was pledged to give military assistance to Poland on any pretext which the Polish Government claimed as a threat to its sovereignty. Warsaw, in other words, was pulling the strings, and Britain, through our Government, was pledged to dance accordingly. Needless to say, this simply encouraged the Polish Government to refuse to discuss Danzig with Germany.

On August 23rd came the non-aggression pact between Germany and the Soviet Union, despite the presence in Moscow of Stafford Cripps who was trying to persuade the Kremlin to enter into a pact with Britain. My reading of the situation again showed an inability to analyse deeper motives. I assumed that since Russia and Germany had undertaken not to attack one another, that no British Government would contemplate war with Germany.

To my astonishment, a move which I thought would make war unlikely was interpreted by the Press and radio in Britain as encouraging the reverse. I now came to the conclusion that it was the Cabinet's purpose to exacerbate an already fraught situation, and that the belligerent attitude of the media was Government-inspired.

Then came the actual declaration of war, and with it the greatest hypocrisy of all. Our Government had guaranteed to "preserve the territorial integrity of Poland" yet when the Soviet army invaded Poland from the East three weeks after the Germans had marched over her Western borders, Britain refrained from declaring war on the Soviets. If we were morally justified in declaring war on Germany we were so bound to do so on Russia.

It took six years of war with millions dead to provide the answer to this question which was that the Anglo-Polish Agreement of 25 August 1939 carried with it a secret protocol restricting the scope of the Agreement to German aggression which was not published until 5 April 1945. The British people had been hood-winked and so had the Poles, for at the end of the day Britain's dud cheques left them ground under the heels of the Red Army.

With the nation at war, it was obvious that my family, living at the local headquarters of a Movement wholly opposed to the war policies of our Government, could easily become the targets of bias and victimisation. It had already been rumoured that we had painted swastikas in the HQ roof so that German bomber crews would make certain we were not bombed, and such absurdities and lies were seriously discussed and believed. So for a few weeks my wife and daughter moved to Southport, returning to Hull when we had succeeded in finding alternative accommodation.

It always surprised me that our continued activities after the outbreak of war did not create more active opposition on the streets.

We continued with our regular "*Action*" paper sales and street meetings aimed at winning popular support for a just and nego-tiated peace. People would still stand and listen but were less inclined now to ask questions. Perhaps they were afraid that their motives might be misconstrued by other listeners in the crowd.

Our sales of *Action* increased slightly but people were more furtive in their approach. I had already lost some of my active members recalled to the armed forces, my treasurer Jim Bellini among them. Both his parents were of Italian birth, but natural-ised British citizens, and Jim was on the army reserve.

I missed him sorely when he went, and never heard of him again. He certainly did not return to Hull and make contact with any of his former associates. This was when Vic King took over as treasurer of the branch, being at the time one of my most active members.

While British Union was not an anti-semitic movement, numbers of our speakers were. To some extent this could be said of me, though my remarks from the platform were always directed against the behaviour of a proportion of Jews, and not attacks on Jews as a whole. My attitude, in fact, was one of response rather than attack, and in the years after the war I was to make a number of Jewish friends in my business life.

There was no mistaking the type of Jewish opponent we were up against in the '30s however. The men who threw me through the Southport shop window in 1933 were Jewish, and it is a matter of record that Jews figured excessively in the convictions for assault on our members, including women and girls. It is also accepted that Lord Rothermere's withdrawal of the Daily Mail editorial support for British Union in the summer of 1934 was brought about by the threatened loss of Jewish advertising. This pattern, it should be noted, was established before Oswald Mosley had as much as referred to Jews in a public speech.

Against this background, it is hardly surprising that by the end of the '30s anti-Jewish feeling became more and more pronounced among our members. Some of our supporters took advantage of blackout conditions to institute a series of covert attacks against certain Jewish-owned shops in the town, in an attempt to relieve their feelings of frustration during the period of the phony war.

I realise that reporting this will not rebound to our credit. These actions were not of a serious character, and consisted of sealing the door locks of the shops with an infusion of plastic wood which overnight would set and thereby prevent the insertion of a key to unlock the door. The locks then had to be sprayed with spirit to dissolve the plastic.

These incidents had been reported to the police. I discovered one night that some of our members had gone into the city centre intent upon a repetition, and I received a 'phone call tipping me off that the police were out in force to catch the culprits.

I immediately set off on my bike and after some time I found three of our members, but they only had one tube of plastic which they had used once.

I took it from them and put it in my pocket. I was about to mount my bike and leave when a number of police officers appeared out of the blackout. One shouted "There's Charnley. Get him, Get him", which they proceeded to do. My bike was left in the street, and I was arrested and taken to the Central Police Station. I had not thought to throw the tube away, and of course my explanation for my possession of it was not believed.

After being detained in a police cell for about three hours I was allowed to go home. My wife already knew from the members who had returned to our headquarters where I was, and was very relieved to see me on my return. I was later charged with malicious damage to property and fined ten pounds.

During this period, the last few months of the 'phoney war',

British Union fought three parliamentary bye-elections, one in the London borough of Silvertown, the others at Middleton, near Manchester, and Leeds. Mosley addressed meetings in all constituencies, but by this time war fever, arising from Government and media propaganda, was beginning to be felt, and our share of the vote was not encouraging.

Prior to the Mosley meeting at Middleton, we were besieged for some considerable time by an angry mob in the local headquarters. Some of the windows were smashed and attempts were made to batter down the door. A telephone call resulted in a relief contingent arriving, and being attacked now from their front, and by our comrades at their rear, the Reds dispersed in considerable confusion.

The candidate at Middleton was 43 year old Frederick Haslam, a local engine designer who had served in the First War in Palestine and France as a sergeant in the Lancashire Fusiliers and Machine Gun Corps. Within weeks of the election he was to find himself imprisoned without charge or trial, his loyalty to his country suspect, and detention continued on the order of Home Secretary Herbert Morrison who was working in an apple orchard as a conscientious objector at the time that Frederick Haslam was winning the Military Medal on the Somme.

At Leeds our candidate was another ex-serviceman, Sydney Allen, an early member of the Movement who had served in the 5th West Yorkshire Regiment in France from September 1914 to December 1918, and who was the largest poultry breeder in the North. My old friend, ex-Royal Navy man, Tommy Moran, was the candidate at Silvertown.

After Mosley's meeting in Leeds, I questioned him about our continued freedom in view of the hotting-up of the war. He told me that there were many historical instances of opposition to war in England, starting with the American War of Independence, The Napoleonic Wars, the Crimean War, the Boer War, and even the

1914-1918 War. Charles James Fox was known to be pro-Napoleon, Lloyd George from parliamentary benches condemned the Boer War, and many present-day Labour Members of Parliament had opposed the 1914-18 war including Ramsey MacDonald and Jimmy Thomas.

Mosley did not, therefore, anticipate any parliamentary action against us because past history had created precedents. What he thought possible was that the Government would officially proscribe the Movement, in which case any future political activity would become illegal.

As a very remote possibility, Mosley envisaged that he and some senior officials might be arrested without prior banning orders against the Movement, and as a prominent speaker, I could anticipate inclusion in this category.

In January 1940 my son Cedric was born, a happy family time which contrasted with the developing world events. The military position on the Continent was looking grim, and there seemed little obvious hope of a negotiated peace. Attitudes were hardening, and the age-old concept of "My country right or wrong" was making our efforts for an honourable peace less and less acceptable to the majority of people. Against this background, Mosley spoke to a great May Day rally and Peace Campaign meeting in our great stronghold of the working people, the streets of East London. How well I remember that occasion!

I was close to the loudspeaker van, and as Mosley approached through the crowd, he came across directly to me instead of heading for the van. He put his hand on my shoulder, gripped it, and said, "Hello Charnley. You here again! These annual meetings wouldn't be complete without you, would they?" I couldn't say a word. I was so filled with emotion. And he knew. He just gave me a gentle shake and that half smile, turned and walked towards the van, before mounting the ladder.

That is the sort of feeling the mass of East Enders felt. I was present at many of the East London meetings, but to try and explain this feeling of euphoria, this incredible rapport that existed between the East Enders and OM, and to a lesser extent between them and Mick Clarke, is impossible. If you try to multiply that feeling by thousands upon thousands, you might get some idea of the atmosphere, the sense of comradeship, the magnetic waves flowing from that man to that audience. The whole atmosphere was alive, vibrant, electrical! There's never been a man like OM. I would have died for him.

My recollections of the final weeks before my arrest are very vague. It is as if a veil had been draw over our final struggle for peace, probably because I was eventually beginning to accept the inevitability of all-out total war, and this to me was anathema.

I do remember one of my final gestures of defiance against the Government. On May 23rd, 1940 Oswald Mosley and a small number of his senior N.H.Q. officials were arrested under newly-passed legislation. Habeus Corpus was suspended, and the Home Secretary was authorised to arrest and imprison any citizen for an indefinite period without charge or trial. This meant the virtual closing down of our headquarters and the cessation of all instructions and directives.

We were on our own. What was I to do? With our national weekly "*Action*" now banned, Vic King and I decided to produce our own news sheet. We had a typewriter and a small duplicating machine, and from these we produced an eight page stapled booklet with a coloured backing, which we entitled 'British Freedom'.

We distributed it as far as Leeds, Grimsby, Lincoln and York. At least we were trying to do something. I cannot recall its contents, but I know I contributed one of the articles. Most were compiled by Vic and Harry Townend, who, I had a reunion in 1983, together with Bill Cromwell, another Hull member.

On my 30th birthday, 1940, just ten years after reading Mosley's resignation speech from MacDonald's government, I received a 'phone call from a friend at the Central Police Station asking me to call there on my way home from work. When I arrived, he told me, in confidence, that I could expect to be arrested within a day or so, and that his son, who was my deputy in the East Hull constituency, would probably be arrested too.

I went home and gave Edith the news. She was not particularly surprised since I had told her of Mosley's foreboding some weeks previously. When Vic came in from work I told him, too, and we agreed there was little that we could do.

Chapter Three

Political Prisoner

ON June 3rd, the police came to my place of work and put me under arrest. My employer shook me emotionally by the hand and thanked me for my years of service. His three sons did likewise and I was driven to my home ostensibly to collect night clothes and toothbrush etc.

I had no idea how long I was likely to be away because I had broken no law and therefore would not be put on trial, and without trial there could be no sentence.

When I arrived home the place was in turmoil. Rose was at school, and Edith naturally upset, but more controlled than I had expected. She was nonetheless enraged at the behaviour of the police. Our home was in a shambles. Drawers had been emptied, the contents scattered around, carpets taken up, lino ripped up and off the flooring, loose floorboards removed. The false ceiling into the cockloft had been pulled down and all my books, private papers, letters, leaflets etc., confiscated. This rampageous search went on after I had arrived home. While I was in our dining room having a cup of tea, a police officer attempted to lift my five-month-old son out of his pram so as to search the well. He wished that he had not done so. My wife threatened to hit him with the poker if he continued, and she would have done so, too.

The sergeant in charge told the officer that this was not necessary. It was a long time before I saw my daughter again. I said my farewells to Edith and was taken to Central Police Station where I was joined by Frank Danby, and a non-active elderly member, Leo Mortell, who in fact had allowed his membership to lapse some years earlier. I had known him, of course, in my early days in Hull but had almost forgotten his existence. Not surprisingly I was astonished to see him.

We were all fingerprinted and taken to Hedon Road Gaol where we were placed in separate cells. Edith brought me a hot meal in the early evening but I was not allowed to see her. We were given no information as to where we were likely to be taken, although we knew that Mosley and the others were at Brixton. I attempted to sleep on a wooden palette and straw mattress with two blankets, but with little success. And so began three-and-a-half years of arbitrary imprisonment, without charge or trial.

Came the dawn, and after a hasty breakfast of skilly, stale bread and margarine, and a mug of a warm muddy liquid masquerading as tea, we were hurried out to a waiting Black Maria, and after being handcuffed together, hustled inside. We were not told of our destination.

After a short journey we were ordered out of the van, and still handcuffed led into Paragon Railway Station. Here we were left in the middle of the railway concourse, where we soon became the centre of attraction to the crowds hurrying to work.

Frank and I were well known by sight, and copies of the previous night's Hull Daily Mail were still on display together with billboards announcing the arrest of the local Fascist Leader. Our police escorts had gone to secure railway tickets for our journey, and were in no hurry to relieve us from our embarrassment.

As I stood in the centre of that milling crowd I began to wonder why we were really there. Not that I was having regrets or second thoughts about my activities over the previous seven years. Regrets or guilty conscience I have never had. The views I held and expressed were sincere and I have never been a pacifist, or avoided conflict as an easy option.

Perhaps for the first time I was concerned as to the behaviour and attitude towards us, of the political establishment in an avoidable war of its own choosing.

According to the Government, one of the reasons we were now at war was to defend free speech, while Germany, in contrast, imprisoned its opponents without regard for legal conventions. Yet I had not been charged with any offence, and was a political prisoner of our own Government.

Only a few weeks before, the Home Secretary, Sir John Anderson, had assured Churchill and his Cabinet, that Mosley and British Union did not constitute in any way a threat or a danger to the realm. Mosley himself had made a statement, published in *Action*, that in the event of Germany invading our country, he and every B.U.F. member would immediately place themselves at the disposal of the authorities for the defence of our country.

Precedents of domestic political opposition to war were numerous. The war against the American Declaration of Independence, the Napoleonic War, the Crimean and Boer Campaigns, and the 1914-18 war; all had their opponents within the United Kingdom. But this was the first time that opponents had been arrested and imprisoned. We were not even aliens, but British citizens, and yet this was happening to Englishmen in England. I asked myself "Where honesty lay and where deceit?" The answer could brook no denial. Churchill was the deceptionist. Mosley was the honest man. I learned the reasons later.

Eventually the policemen returned and we joined the train. Shortly after leaving the station we were told that we were bound for Liverpool, and Walton Gaol.

I had known its exterior for a number of years, owing to Liverpool's close proximity to Southport, and its grim facade did nothing to brighten future prospects. At least we could be fairly sure that many other Mosley supporters would be joining us there. I had done this journey so many times in the past that I recognised every station we passed through, but could not help wondering how long it would be before I made a return journey.

Sweeping military successes had ensured Germany's mastery of continental Europe, but now that the possibility of a negotiated peace had faded, only an invasion of Britain could ensure final victory for Germany, and invasion would be a military gamble on the grandest scale.

Not since William of Normandy had victory gone to the aspiring invader, and in any case I did not relish the thought of German occupation. My mind was in turmoil. I could not accept the humiliation of military defeat, but my instinct was still to oppose the war, and I could not bring myself to look forward with any degree of anticipation to a Churchill triumph.

Leo Mortell was sunk in silent introspection. He could not understand why he had been arrested, a sense of bewilderment which I shared. Frank Danby and I had at least been active in our opposition to the war but Mortell had expressed no political interest for years.

I never found out who was responsible for preparing the original list of detainees, and there were to be a number of later arrests of Hull members who joined me in Walton in the following weeks.

Even Frank had little to say. Recently married he must have been concerned for the safety of his wife since it could be anticipated that as the war hotted up Hull would become a major target for enemy bombers. And so it proved — more than 80,000 houses were destroyed or damaged and 120,000 people made homeless. We had previously agreed that Edith and our children would return to Southport.

Finally we arrived in Liverpool, a station to whose familiar surroundings I had never anticipated returning in handcuffs. I was tempted to inquire about the leg-irons, but for once discretion over-ruled my impetuosity. We were unceremoniously hustled off the train, again in full view of the public and into a Black Maria and on to Walton Prison.

As we pulled outside the huge double gates, I noticed one of the numerous government propaganda posters on the official notice board. It read: "Lend To Defend The Right To Be Free". My last free expression was to draw the attention of the two policemen to its hypocritical absurdity. They made no comment but were quite obviously embarrassed. I knew them both by sight as they had often stood on duty at my open-air meetings. I discovered later that the same poster was also prominently displayed outside Brixton Gaol.

We drove through the gates, and as we got out of the Black Maria we were surrounded by a milling crowd of shouting men, many of whom I had known for years.

The first man I spoke to was Jorian Jenks, an outstanding personality in the Movement, our Agricultural expert, who regularly contributed to *Action* and was in the main the author of our policy in this field.

He and Mosley were farming contemporaries, Mosley coming from a farming background with roots deep in the Staffordshire soil. We had been friends for many years and Jorian had often stayed with me in Hull, which though a port primarily concerned with fish and timber, had a large agricultural hinterland for which I was responsible.

Jorian was quite despondent, and was the first to openly express the view that the war would last for many years. I was surprised to see him in Walton, since I had expected that, as a leading member, he would have been taken to Brixton. He explained however, that he had been living on his smallholding in South Wales which was nearer to Liverpool than London.

I have little recollection of the individuals who I met, they were so numerous and the time so hectic that nothing seemed to make any lasting impression. I know that more and more political friends were arriving every few minutes and it was obvious that the prison officers were ill-prepared for our huge numbers.

Eventually we were herded into the prison-proper and locked into individual cells no larger than a public toilet and containing nothing more than a wooden seat that stretched wall to wall. After what seemed hours, we were given a meal of sorts. Although I cannot recall what it consisted of, I do remember though that I could not eat it, but I did manage to drink what purported to be tea.

After another long wait we were taken in batches of twenty-five or so to the main wings of the prison. These consisted of five double-sided landings, each containing about eighteen cells. I was taken up to No. 5 platform, and was the last to be put into a cell, No. C5/35. Access to the landings was by iron spiral stairway or a series of stairways at the opposite end of the wing to my cell. Here there were huge windows from ground floor to ceiling, draped with huge black curtains in compliance with the black-out regulations.

The landings were about two yards in width which allowed just enough room for two people to pass. These were guarded by iron balustrades about four feet high, just high enough to deter would-be suicide jumpers. Wire mesh of some obvious strength was stretched from side to side.

The cell measured roughly ten feet by five and contained a bedboard against a wall, draped with two rough blankets. There were no sheets, but in front of the bedboard was a mattress which appeared to be stuffed with coarse horsehair, and extremely hard. There was also a pillow filled with the same type of filling but without a pillow case. In one corner was a small triangular wooden fixture on which was a washbowl and water jug, and below on a shelf an enamel badly-chipped chamber pot with battered lid, its interior heavily encrusted with urine rime.

In another corner was a wooden four-legged table on which

was placed a Bible, and in front a hard-bottomed wooden chair. On the wall above was a small wooden-framed mirror, with the number of another cell on the back in coloured crayon. When I left Walton for Ascot camp some time later I took it with me as a souvenir. I still have it today.

High up on the wall opposite the door was a deep embrasured window of small panes of glass, one section of which could be opened, and indeed must have been open for some considerable time. There were hundreds of pigeons around the body of the prison, and as this wing had not been in use for many years, many of the cells had been used for nesting.

Mine was in a filthy state, the floor inches thick in pigeon droppings. It stank, and my first wish on my appreciation of this degradation of the human spirit and humiliation of the body was to mete out similar treatment to Winston Churchill. I have loathed him from that moment. I am sure that the Boers did not treat him in this manner when he was held as a prisoner of war, though as an armed civilian, they would have been perfectly justified in shooting him. A Bible and a filthy chamber pot — typically Churchill!

Some time after being put in the cell, the door was unlocked and I was supplied with a mug of warm cocoa which proved quite palatable, despite an inordinate amount of cocoa butter swimming on the surface.

I learned later to skim this off and found that it could be used as a makeshift nightlight. All that was required was a piece of string and suitable container to hold the fat. In the days ahead I was to read for many hours by this means after the cell lights had been extinguished.

When that cell door slammed shut you realised the solitariness of your fate. Strong men broke under the strain. One of my own members, who was later arrested and brought to Walton, banged on his door and cried on his first night of prison. His name? Jim Humphries, an ex-serviceman of the First World War, decorated for bravery with the M.C. and the Croix de Guerre. He was quite typical of Mosley's supporters. He had known the war of the trenches, and wanted peace, so he joined British Union. But Churchill wanted war, and he got it and at what a cost.

I undressed, lay on the mattress, covered myself with the blankets, and to my surprise fell asleep, but it was a sleep disjointed and troubled. In the early hours I was awakened by a knocking on the cell door. Back in Hull we had a neighbour, who to say the least, was anti-Mosley, a prison warder, employed at the local Hedon Road Gaol. My cell door opened, and to my amazement it was my one-time neighbour, come to vent his vituperative spleen upon me.

"Now we've got you, you Fascist bastard, we'll put you up against a wall and shoot you any day now. All bloody traitors should be shot. We are only waiting for our orders. It might even be tomorrow. I hope I get the chance of shooting you".

The door shut, and then silence. The sudden influx of hundreds of detainees had caused many prison officers to be transferred to Walton, hence his presence at my cell door. I had no reason to know that he was merely taunting me, although I suspected that he was. Even so my mind was troubled, and there was little sleep after that. I was glad when the sound of activity announced the beginning of prison life proper.

Each prison day began with the opening of the cell door, followed by the 'pee pee parade', when you lined up outside your door with a water jug in one hand and a jerry in the other.

Two lines of inmates advanced towards the centre of the landing into a recess containing toilets, with water taps over huge metal sinks. The pattern was to empty the pot down the sluice, clean it as best you could in cold water, then fill the water jug and return to your cell. Cell doors were left open until after the serving of breakfast, which consisted of thick glutinous porridge often containing mouse droppings, two slices of bread and a pot of margarine, some salt in a small pot, and a mug of foul tea.

Fortunately from early youth I had been accustomed to porridge for breakfast, so this for me was not too much of an ordeal and I even came to accept the true Scottish way, salt instead of sugar. I also found other uses for the porridge; I used it to stick a small snapshot of my wife and children to the wall of my cell, the evidence still visible on the back of the photograph today.

For the first week or ten days we were not allowed to write any letters, and so were completely out of contact with relatives or friends. During this early period we were locked up for twenty-three hours a day, with a brief exercise in the yard in the morning and again in the afternoon.

If the weather was bad we walked around the landing in a constantly repeated circle, during which we were forbidden to speak to anyone.

This early rule even applied when we were in the exercise yard. Perhaps they thought we might plan the overthrow of the Government, but like all bureaucratic behaviour it was stupid and only tended to make us more uncooperative.

One day, we were given a letter form on prison notepaper, and from then on could send as many letters as we wished, though were only allowed to receive one a week. Needless to say outgoing and incoming letters were censored. We were now also allowed a weekly visit, usually limited to two people, but children were not permitted.

All attempts to make contact with other inmates during the hours the cell doors were locked were strictly forbidden, with penalties for those found to be breaking the rules. There was never hot water for washing or shaving, and I knew from experience that to shave in cold water brought out a rash on my face so I decided not to shave until I was released, a self-imposition to which I kept.

From this time we were also allowed 'free association', which meant that cell doors remained open during the entire day and mailbag sewing could be undertaken, if desired.

The maximum that could be earned was three shillings a week, which was credited to the detainee's account. I had always been handy with a needle (and still am) and I chose to do some sewing as an alternative to boredom.

One day the sluices became blocked at the time of slopping out and overflowed. The stench was appalling, the effluent over-flowing the landing and on to the landings below. It was some hours before the blockage was cleared and during this time we were allowed to walk around the exercise yard.

The weather in the summer and autumn of 1940 was beautiful and it was galling to be locked up in that foul building, espe-cially during long summer evenings. We found that by standing on the movable table we could look out of the window, and with the aid of a small mirror outside could see and talk to others in close proximity to one's own cell.

This practise was severely frowned upon, and in fact on occa-sion even merited withdrawal of normal food and the substi-tution of bread and water, with a spell in the punishment cells below ground. Not an enjoyable experience I can assure you. We also found that by putting a weighted end to a wax-strengthened mailbag thread, we could, by using the pendulum technique, pass messages and small objects from one floor to another. Some of us became quite expert at this method of communication. One Yorkshire member caught in this practise was brought before the governor and sentenced to three days bread and water.

Fortunately, Edith had returned to Southport, and I received visits from her every Saturday. She was often accompanied by one of her sisters who had been one of my early dancing partners before my involvement with politics. My children came also, but I was not allowed to see them, and they had to remain in reception. Visits scheduled for half an hour seemed to last no more than ten minutes.

We were in Walton about eight weeks before being moved to the camp at Ascot, but shortly before this, those in my age group liable for National Service were told to report to the governor's office. There were seven of us, but I remember only one, Charlie Dickinson, one of the Manchester members, who I had known from my very early days.

He had, on more than one occasion, accompanied Tommy Moran on his visits to Southport and Ormskirk in 1934. I told the others that I had no intention of registering, my argument being that as a political prisoner, unjustly deprived of my liberty, I was under no obligation to do so. Most of the others said that they would adopt the same line but I don't know if they did.

When it came to my turn I was confronted by the governor sitting at his desk, and two other men, one in military uniform, the other in civilian clothes, probably a civil servant from the Ministry of Labour and National Service. I answered questions regarding my name, age, religion, nationality, but when it came to my address I said: "His Majesty's Prison, Liverpool", which rather startled them. They did not appreciate that I was being perfectly truthful. I had no home address. My home in Hull had been vacated, my furniture was in store, and Edith and children were living with my mother-in-law. I greatly appreciated their discomfit. They then asked me the address of my wife and I refused to give it, saying that it was not their prerogative to know.

I was asked which of the armed services I was prepared to join, given a preference. I declined to answer. They then requested me to sign, placing the national service paper before me. I replied that I had no intention of signing. This amazed them. I think I must have been the first to adopt this attitude. They collectively told me that I had to sign, that everybody in the country was required to sign for national service when their age group came up. I again refused and said that, instead, I wanted to make a statement, which they agreed. My statement was: "I am a loyal British subject. I have been arrested and imprisoned in defiance of Magna Carta which guaranteed that no British subject would be arrested and subjected to imprisonment without being charged with an offence and tried. When you and your Government release me from imprisonment, then I will decide whether or not to sign for national service, but certainly not while I am being held as a prisoner".

While we were still in Walton Vic King and Jim Humphries were both detained and brought in. I had received a message with my breakfast one morning that two more members had arrived from Hull. I was naturally anxious to see them, and sent a message back asking them to attend the C of E church parade on Sunday. Those who wished could always attend Sunday service and I had in the past attended Mass. The death penalty for murder was still being carried out, and we were told on one occasion that in a specially hooded box at the front of the church was a man awaiting execution. When later the dreaded moment of execution took place a strange thing happened. Every prisoner throughout the gaol was aware of what was happening because immediately after the serving of breakfast all cell doors were locked. At a few minutes before eight o'clock there rose an increasing roar of sound — everybody was banging on the door of the cell with some object, usually the feet of his chair. Just as suddenly the noise stopped. It was unnerving in its intensity.

But back to the church parade. All I had to do to contact my friends was to join the Anglican service instead of going to Mass. I knew that the service would not be unfamiliar and that I was almost certain to know the hymns. As I walked down the centre aisle I noticed Vic at the end of a pew, and as I reached him, he moved over to give me room. We did not spend much time on our devotions but rather in friendly chatter. He cheered me, especially since we had been told that we would probably be leaving Walton soon for a camp where we would all be together with more freedom of movement. One thing I remember of the service. The minister, very unwisely, chose for one of his hymns that which was sung to the tune of the German national anthem, and since there were also many Anglo-Germans detained under 18b, they sang Deutschland-Deutschland, uber alles, with great gusto, to the embarrassing chagrin of the minister. The prison officers who were with us in the church were completely powerless to do anything about it.

On the whole the food in Walton was very poor. I often suspected that the food for 18b prisoners was sabotaged before it left the kitchen, perhaps with the approval of some of the prison officers who were openly hostile towards us.

In the first few days of our imprisonment we were often told that firing squads were expected to arrive at the prison any day to carry out our executions. We were even shown the wall in the exercise yard against which we were to be lined up to be shot. When we received boiled potatoes with our midday meal it was obvious that they had been neither washed or peeled, and it was a common occurrence for many cockroaches to be found in a variety of dishes, especially boiled rice.

One officer took a delight in telling us that he had ordered the prison kitchen staff to sweep up the cockroaches from the dark corners of the kitchen and to dump them into our food. I once complained to the governor about cockroaches in the food only to be told that my complaints were both mischievous and frivolous.

By the time we were allowed to receive visitors we could also accept food parcels from them, and these helped considerably to improve our overall diet. I was fortunate in that Edith was a qualified confectioner-pastry-cook and so I probably fared better than most.

It would be nearing the end of July when we were told we were to be moved to a detention camp. Though its whereabouts was not given, I was so relieved to be leaving Walton that the circumstances of our departure made no lasting impression on my mind. I remember teaming up with Vic King and Jim Humphries shortly after being entrained from Lime Street Station, and being told that our destination was a short distance from London. Leo Mortell had been released after only a few weeks detention and I was pleased that at least one stupidity had been rectified. I never saw him again, and do not know if he even survived the war.

We left Walton in the early hours and by mid-afternoon, after a short tramp from Ascot railway station, found ourselves inside the barbed wire perimeter of the racecourse which had been turned into one of Britain's wartime concentration camps.

After a lengthy wait we were addressed by an Army colonel, plainly embarrassed to find himself the commandant of a camp containing so many Englishmen, many of whom were ex-servicemen of the First World War, of varying rank, and carrying many medals of distinction.

We had a British Admiral, Sir Barry Domvile, K.B.E., C.B., C.M.G., a former Admiral of the Imperial Russian Navy, various colonels and majors, captains and lieutenants almost by the score.

He told us, with apparent sincerity, that he would make our stay as pleasant as his orders would permit, that we would be allowed a large measure of internal freedom; that internal discipline was for us to agree and operate; and that we must elect our own camp leader who would act as intermediary on our behalf.

We were to be housed in large huts and canvas tents, each hut having its own elected leader. He required twelve volunteers for kitchen duty, who would draw rations each day from the quartermaster and be responsible for the preparation of all meals.

Vic and I volunteered immediately for the kitchen, and soon got our dozen volunteers, one of whom was an Anglo-German, Arthur Lechscheid, who I met on a number of occasions in London after the war.

Arthur was the son of a First World War POW who had chosen to remain in England, married an English girl, and had a small bakery business in East London. After release from detention in 1943 he rejoined his father's business, but later left him to run a pub cum restaurant. Alas my post war London visits were too fully occupied with meetings, and I lost touch with him. As a German national he had been eligible for, and had joined, the Hitler Jugend. For this he was detained under 18b. During the later years of the war my brother Syd did a lot of contract bakery work in London, sometimes working for Lechschied senior, and meeting his son.

We had an excellent chef in charge of the kitchen in the person of Rudi Rottensteiner. An Austrian, he also had been a prisoner of war back in 1917, had married an English girl, became naturalised and legally changed his name to Rothwell. He had a son, who in 1940 was a university student without (or so he claimed) any political affiliations. Both father and son were arrested under the name of Rottensteiner, even though the son was born after his father's change of name and his birth registered in the name of Rothwell. Throughout the whole of the time that I knew them in the camps they were always called and known as Rottensteiner.

Our first task in the kitchen was to prepare a hasty meal, while other detainees were getting settled into camp life. There were three main huts, the Anglo-Germans gravitating towards one, the politicals, most of whom were British Union, occupying the other two, while the greater bulk of the Italians were accommodated in the bell tents. Before the war the camp had been the winter quarters for Bertram Mills Circus.

The original kitchen staff soon ran into difficulties in satisfying the demands of the detainees. I think there were between six and seven hundred in the camp, some three hundred more than the camp commandant had expected — hence the use of the tents. The paramount problem was that the camp was only receiving rations to supply four hundred inmates, and with the exception of bread, which we could get in plenty, the remaining rations had to be extended to almost double that number. To make matters worse we were told that according to the Geneva Convention, prisoners of war were only entitled to half the rations of a serving soldier, and since we were now under military authority our conditions came under military ruling.

This made the problem of feeding the men more difficult than ever. Because of the speed at which the government departments work, it was nearly two months before the camp received reasonable quantities of food, but human nature being what it is, there were inevitable rumours that the kitchen staff were holding back supplies, operating a black market or eating additional food at the expense of everyone else. After a number of heated arguments, all the kitchen staff walked out, and a new crowd took over, but with the retention of the same head cook, Rudi Rottensteiner.

So I vacated the bunkhouse where the kitchen staff had been bedded down and moved into E room, where I was asked to assume the position of room leader, responsible to the camp leader Tommy Moran for general cleanliness, tidiness and collective complaints. Sleeping arrangements were in three-tier bunks, with a canvas palliasse stuffed with straw, two rough cotton sheets and a bolster with cotton cover.

Each prisoner was responsible for maintaining the cleanliness of their bedding. Toilet facilities were primitive in the extreme, except that body refuse and washing waters plus kitchen waste was all directed into piping which in turn emptied into a huge septic tank.

The camp was provided with a large compound with administrative officers and army personnel accommodation outside the main camp perimeter, which was compounded of double barbed-wire fencing. The camp leader was daily briefed by the officer of the day but could see the camp commandant on request, all individual requests by detainees going through the camp leader. We had a huge room which could be used for a variety of purposes including various forms of entertainment, for example concerts, of which we had quite a few; lectures; boxing and wrestling bouts, with, on one occasion, a friendly boxing contest between ex-British Heavyweight champion Joe Beckett and ex-naval Middleweight champion, Tommy Moran.

I took part in two concerts, once as a member of a group singing western songs. 'Home on the Range' — 'The Black Hills of Dakota', and similar items, and once as a soloist when one of my songs was 'The Lincolnshire Poacher'.

There were two pianos in this room and our two detainee concert pianists made regular use of them in daily practice. One was Jim Battersby, son of the well-known firm of hatters of Stockport, who I met frequently in Southport in the immediate post-war years. Alas he came to a tragic and untimely end. The other was an Anglo-German whose name I cannot remember. One of his favourite selections was 'Eine Kleine Nacht Musik', and it afterwards became one of mine. I seldom hear it played without being transported back to Ascot Camp and those turbulent times during The Battle of Britain. We were sufficiently near London to often see the aerial combats in the distant sky.

A number of Anglo-Germans were members of British Union and in many instances it was their membership that had been responsible for their detention. To a lesser extent this could also be said of the Anglo-Italians, although the majority of these had been more closely allied to Italian influences, many belonging to the Fascio di Londra. We were in consequence a mixed bunch with what might legitimately be called mixed loyalties, and yet throughout the whole period of my detention I never experienced or heard of any antagonisms or hostility between the various groups.

Only once did I see any expression of concern among the Italian contingent and that was when news filtered through of the downfall of Mussolini. The majority of them were positively stunned and overwhelmed by the news. In the end they were more loyal to their leader than their own nationals in Italy.

The Anglo-Germans behaved differently. They followed the fortunes of the German armies in Russia and North Africa with avid interest, and Rommel's reverses at Alamein, followed by the long retreat, had a sobering effect upon them. The final collapse at Stalingrad and the surrender of Von Paulus was a shattering blow, and from then on there was a change in their usual exuberance.

Feelings were kept more under control and few comments were made, but the possibility of ultimate defeat for the Axis began to be contemplated. Yet, throughout these traumatic years and the early defeats of the British Armed Forces, never once did I see any evoked expression of animosity or hostility that might have been expected in such a mixed camp.

It was a long hot summer and time passed very slowly. Rumour and counter-rumour spread throughout the camp as to our ultimate destination and fate. Many detainees of varying origins and nationalities had already been transported to Canada. At the beginning of July, a U-boat had torpedoed the Arandora Star and a thousand German and Italian internees had lost their lives and the legality of transporting British political detainees beyond our shores was often debated. The legal argument fell because our very detention was itself a denial of Magna Carta. If Churchill could flout Magna Carta by imprisoning us there was no reason to believe that he would not do so again if it suited his purpose.

Many inmates received visitors during the summer and we could see them outside the barbed wire close by the room where visits were held. They were not supposed to speak to us but at least they could wave. I did not receive any visits during my stay at Ascot. Travel was not easy with wartime restrictions and in any case my wife could afford neither the time nor the cost. Without income, she had had to find work soon after my arrest, and there were two children to feed in addition to caring for herself.

One visitor I do recall was Tommy Moran's wife, Toni, I had known her from my very early days in the Movement as Mrs Sharpe, before she and Tommy married. Toni was a very forceful speaker and well-known in and around Manchester for her vicious tongue in repartee.

She was notoriously anti-Semitic, and barracked by a Jew while speaking, would unloose a torrent of abuse in Yiddish that would literally blast the interrupter into stunned silence.

Shortly after our arrival at Ascot the Government appointed appeals tribunals began their hearings. These were held in London, and always followed a pattern. The panel consisted of three, with a chairman usually a King's Counsel, Sir Norman Birkett and Derek Curtis-Bennett being among the better known.

Their task was to cross-examine the detainee during a question and answer session with, if possible, an extended voluntary state-ment from the prisoner. After the hearing the chairman would make a recommendation to the Home Secretary concerning the advisability or otherwise of release. Herbert Morrison was under no obligation to accept the recommendation, nor was the indi-vidual ever informed of the results, and this First War conscientious objector generally ignored these recommendations.

The detainee was supplied with a list of so-called reasons for his detention a few days before the hearing, which in some instances were very brief, while others might last hours with the experience quite traumatic.

In the late summer of 1940 I was taken to London for my first tribunal hearing, replete with a duplicated sheet of foolscap giving the reasons for my detention. These were:-

- That I was a member of a political party the aims and objects of which were similar to those of the Government of a country with which His Majesty's Government was at war.

- That there was reasonable cause to believe that my actions might be detrimental to the successful projection of the war and that,

- In the opinion of the Home Secretary it was necessary to exercise control over me.

I had therefore been placed under detention. It would sometimes be weeks before the Home Secretary's decision reached the detainee, and in the meantime one was left like a criminal awaiting a jury's verdict. Those freed would be informed at roll call on the morning of release, told to pack their belongings and report to the gate.

The chairman of my tribunal was Derek Curtis-Bennett. He told me that the purpose of the hearing was to decide if he could recommend to the Home Secretary that I be released from detention. The questioning lasted for five hours with a break for lunch.

Curtis-Bennett sat at a table with one other person. I was placed on a hard-bottomed chair about five yards distant from the table. Seated some distance away from the table at an angle to myself, was a fourth figure, and to see him clearly I had to look away from the table. He did not ask any questions at all, nor did he move from his chair which was considerably more comfortable than mine. My posterior has never been well-upholstered.

None of the questions was involved or devious. Why did I join the B.U.F.? When had I joined? Was I anti-Jewish? If I was not, why had I said such and such at a meeting in Hull in 1936? Did I say so-and-so at a meeting in Baker Street? What did I think of Hitler? Did I agree with the actions of Mussolini in Abyssinia? Who did I want to win the war? Was it right for Laval to collaborate with the German occupation forces in France? Was my brother-in-law anti-Semitic? When did I meet Mosley? What did I think of him? How long had I known that Lord Haw-Haw was William Joyce? Did I enjoy listening to his broadcasts from Deutschlandsender? Who did I think would win the war? Did I like Mr. Churchill? If I was released would I volunteer for the armed forces? Did I think that I was mistaken in not registering for national service when I had the opportunity? Curtis-Bennett then made a brief statement, and the gist of what he said was that so far as he was concerned he did not consider me to be a security risk, that he did not question either my loyalty or my patriotism but that unfortunately my brand of patriotism differed greatly from that of the Home Secretary.

Finally, he asked me if I had any regrets regarding my past beliefs and behaviour. Before answering I opened my jacket and shirt and said, "You will not see any feet growing out of my belly. When I am released I will walk out with head high, I will never crawl out, and as to regrets, yes, I have one very large regret". Then I paused, and he said, "Well, what is it?" and I replied, "My eternal regret will be that I did not do more when I had the chance to help Mosley to prevent this war. That is my one regret". And with that my hearing came to an end. Some weeks later I was informed that the Home Secretary could not see his way to authorise my release from detention. As the ex-conscientious objector, Herbert Morrison, had just been appointed Home Secretary, I was not surprised.

18b Prisoners detained on Isle of Man including a Blackshirt vicar. The photograph was smuggled out of the camp by a former Blackshirt District Leader who was serving in the RAF on the island and who later was to win the DFC.

I have sometimes wondered if I was too inconsiderate of my wife and too little concerned with the welfare of my children in declining to temper my views with discretion at the hearing.

I will never know the answer to this one. I am what I am. One thing I am not is a hypocrite. If I had behaved dishonourably when answering questions I would have been eternally at war with my own conscience.

Edith knows that if I had adopted a different course of action I could at least have assisted towards a different decision by Morrison, but she had never upbraided me or condemned me in any way. She had known me for many years before we married and she knew, when she married me, that I was a 'died in the wool' Mosley man.

It is a subject that has never arisen between us since the day I arrived home. Neither of my children has ever expressed any feelings of condemnation against me for my life-long support for Mosley, in fact my son is almost a post-war supporter of my attitude, and it is really at his earnest request that I finally made my decision to write this story, which I began in his home in Perth, Western Australia.

I remember the first inmate of Ascot camp to be called to a Tribunal Hearing — the distinguished anthropologist and former Royal Dragoon Captain, George Henry Lane Fox Pitt-Rivers. By way of registering a protest against his arrest, he refused to report to the gate as he had been instructed.

All attempts by the army authorities to persuade him failed and eventually he was removed from the camp by force, while he continued to express his attitude by passive resistance.

Finally he was dragged ignominiously through the camp gates by two soldiers and forcibly placed in the army truck that took him away.

During this disgraceful treatment, the camp was in an uproar with abuse hurled at the soldiers who carried out the manhandling and at the authorities in general. I was to remember this event when much later in the Isle of Man I was personally involved in a disturbance.

This brings me to what was quite a common practice among some members of the military. After a week or so in Ascot camp, parcels began to arrive for the detainees. They were always very welcome, especially if they contained items of food or cigarettes.

Recipients of parcels were always informed of their arrival which had to be collected from the parcels office and opened in the presence of a scrutineer, usually a sergeant but always with an officer present.

Parcels were often deliberately dropped on the floor before being handed over to be opened. Many were brought by visitors, and frequently contained breakable items such as jars of jam or pickles.

To open a parcel in front of a grinning soldier to find food, and cigarettes, and jam, and broken glass in a jumbled mess was at times stretching nerves to the limit. This is no exaggeration. I saw it happen on more than one occasion when I had been collecting a parcel from my wife. These always came by post so did not contain any glass, but I have had cakes broken to crumbs and mixed up with items of clothing and cigarettes. Wartime enhances the savagery and the brutality of the human psyche.

If this is what the British soldier could do to his own, it is easy to imagine what could happen to the enemy, and conversely what an enemy could do to us. The Germans were not the only sadists in the European theatre of war. We also had our own.

Before the end of that summer Tommy Moran had been to a tribunal and shortly after released. Most of us were surprised at this decision by the authorities. Perhaps it was done deliberately to cause disaffection among the British Union detainees.

I asked Tommy after the war how he accounted for it but he professed ignorance, saying only that his wife had made a nuisance of herself through her Member of Parliament, and this may have had some effect. I would have expected that Toni Moran would have been in Holloway with other, much less active women members, but there was no rhyme or reason in the list of those detained. In Hull we had two sisters in the Movement, one of whom was particularly active and was excellent as a woman steward at noisy meetings, but she was not even questioned by the police, while the inoffensive and lapsed Leo Mortell was put in Walton along with me.

Tommy's departure meant that we had to elect a new camp leader, and we chose the well-known and very urbane and gentlemanly Arthur Swan of Lowestoft. He made an excellent camp leader, having the confidence of every section of the camp's inmates, and was well liked by the Italians, many of whom were quite young.

Not all the Italians were under canvas. I had one 15 year old boy in my room, and he was taking his detention very hard. His father had died some years before, and he had an English mother. An only child, he had the same first name as his father and I often suspected that with their usual bureaucratic efficiency, the authorities had issued a detention order not knowing that the father of the same name had died. I could sometimes hear him crying at night, unable to sleep and probably thinking of his mother alone in London. I would get out of bed and talk to him in an effort to quieten his fears. I was happy for him when he was released. I think it was finally appreciated that a mistake had been made. When he went he gave me a small clock as a parting gift. I still see his tearful face in the dim morning light. His name comes back to me. It was Di Campi.

As I write, more and more events arise from the mists of the past, nudging my memory from its stagnant sleep. I recall that only one self-confessed communist was ever detained under 18b, despite Russia's early alliance with Germany.

He made no secret of his political views and we found it strange that he should be in the same predicament as ourselves. As he was domiciled in my room I came to know him quite well. He was from Sheffield and had been critical of the Hitler-Stalin Pact. He held the view that there was something not quite genuine in this coming together of political opposites and inferred that the presence of Stafford Cripps in Moscow at the time of the announcement of this pact between Russia and Germany had many undertones which would become obvious as the war progressed.

Openly anti-Stalin and pro-Trotsky, he was convinced that this Russian-German pact was only a charade to cloak more long-term secret objectives. He believed that the open expression of these opinions was viewed by the government as detrimental to the achievement of the ultimate goal. Much to our mutual surprise he did not meet with any deliberate hostility from his British Union fellow-detainees.

When we left Ascot we were split into two sections, some going to Huyton, and the remainder to a camp at York. I think it was from York that he was subsequently released, by which time Russia and Germany were at war. He firmly believed that the British Government knew in advance that as German troops invaded Poland from the west, Russian troops would make an attack from the east and that it had been agreed between Stalin and Stafford Cripps that Britain would take no action against Russia. If there was foundation for this theory then numerous long-term possibilities are opened up for conjecture which might provide some answers to the many questions which I and no doubt many others have posed ever since.

Another outstanding personality of the Ascot camp was an Anglo-Italian from Manchester, Dom Rea. He was dark-complexioned with an almost Douglas Fairbanks appearance. An accomplished accordionist with a deep baritone voice, he had his own Italian accordion band in Manchester. He reminded me of the singing troubadours of early European times, as he strolled around the compound singing and playing. One of his favourites was 'O Solo Mia', and another was 'Sorrento', which he would sing in both Italian and English.

One remarkable government vagary was the imprisonment in our camp of a number of Jews, a co-habitation that might be expected to have led to trouble. This was not the case. True they were to some extent ostracised, but they were not subject to any deliberate hostility. If any are still alive, I am sure they would confirm this. I almost felt sorry for the Sellmans, father and son, with the father, who was quite elderly, also partially blind. It was embarrassing to notice the pathetic efforts of Sellman junior to do nothing which might cause annoyance or give offence. I think they must have been either released or moved to another camp, as I do not remember them at Huyton, which was our last camp on the mainland before being moved to the Isle of Man.

Bobby Rietti, whose parents had lived in Italy, was also Jewish and had been interned along with his brother. I did not know him well, but I was told that after his release he found employment as an actor with the B.B.C., and in later years, long after the war, the name of Bobby Rietti often appeared in a variety of programmes. Among other Jews were two diamond merchants, Lipschitz and Kuchinsky, and a very charming South African, Gloster, who made lasting friendships with some B.U.F. members.

For warmth in the winter months we had a series of wood burning stoves which were reasonably efficient, but hot water for the kitchen and the wash-rooms was provided from a large coke-fired boiler. This was situated in the huge room used for various entertainments. It was quite a large furnace and without knowledgeable attention soon became blocked with clinker and incapable of providing the water required. As I had been accustomed to the use of coke-fired bakery ovens I was entrusted with the task of attending it.

For those who wished, there were opportunities of doing farm or forestry work outside the camp. Volunteers lined up at the main gate each morning and marched to their place of work under military guard. I was quite content with the job I had, and this also provided me with opportunities of listening to one of our concert pianists at practise. During those months at Ascot I became familiar with numerous piano concertos although I knew few of them by name and regrettably could not identify them. Joyous listening however did relieve the tedium of those long days. To hear them today can still propel me back in time and I can see the dark head of the pianist bent over the keyboard.

As winter approached, I began to be plagued with bouts of severe constipation and colic, compounded by haemorrhoids, but received little medical attention from the authorities. Many years later I was to require surgery to repair the damage brought about through this studied lack of medical care.

The New Year of 1941 began with heavy falls of snow, and one day, while exercising in the compound, I fell heavily on the ice breaking my right wrist. The pain was very severe. I have had broken bones since, plus a serious car accident, but no pain was ever as bad as this. I was taken to the camp hospital where an orderly put my arm into a temporary splint and told me that I should have to wait until the following day before I could be taken to the military hospital at Aldershot.

On arriving there I asked for something to ease the pain but was bluntly refused by the doctor when told that I was from the detainee's camp. Since the war I have been the recipient of numerous instances of medical care and I have nothing but praise for the dedication so unstintingly lavished upon me. Aldershot hospital was just another instance of the brutalising effect of war.

When the wrist was finally x-rayed, a multiple fracture was diagnosed. I was taken to the theatre where I was anaesthetised and the wrist set and put in plaster from the finger tips to the elbow. After twelve weeks I returned to the hospital for the removal of the plaster, after which the wrist was again x-rayed.

To the amazement of the surgeon, the bones had not knitted together and he diagnosed a serious calcium deficiency in the camp diet as applied to my own particular needs. The wrist was again put in plaster but this time only half-way up the arm and I was told to gently move the tips of my fingers. This surgeon also wrote a letter to the camp medical officer requesting that I be given a daily pint of milk, the milk supplied to the camp kitchen being reconstituted from dried skimmed milk. The surgeon told me that it was doubtful that I would regain the full use of my hand and fingers, but I was determined that when the plaster was finally removed, I would do my utmost to disprove his forecast.

Three weeks later we were moved from Ascot, some of us going to Huyton, Liverpool, others to a camp erected under the stands at York racecourse. I went to Huyton, but all my Hull friends went to York. One of our Hull detainees was Frank Danby.

AFTER LIGHTS OUT   YORK 1 FEB 41

The frendships we have made here and in jail have brightened the darkest days
of these dreary months. These freidships and the high ideals, the firm resolve,
we share, will endure.

York Racecourse Concentration Camp — painted by 18b detainee Rafe Temple Cotton, British Union Devon District Inspector and Parliamentary Candidate for Exeter.

At the time of our arrest, Frank's wife was expecting their first child. They had not long been married and Olga was one of our women members. Olga was living with Frank's parents, but shortly after the birth of the baby Mr. Danby arranged for the family to go and stay for a time with his brother in Belfast. While

116

they were there Belfast received a visit from German bombers, and Frank's mother, wife, child, father, his aunt and uncle, were all killed.

The Home Secretary magnanimously agreed that Frank should be allowed out of detention to attend the funeral of his family. His brother John, British Union's District Leader of Kingston-upon-Thames, now in the Army, was given compassionate leave also to attend.

Frank went to his family funeral *in handcuffs*. He was never the same again. Shortly after, he was released and went to live with his sister-in-law in Kingston-upon-Thames. Later in the war his brother was killed and Frank married his sister-in-law and went to live in Derby. I was given his address by a local member whom I met at a meeting I arranged for Oswald Mosley at the Midland Hotel, Manchester. I went to Derby to see Frank, but unfortunately he was on night work and was not available. I wrote to him a couple of times but received no reply. He had lost all interest in politics, and who could blame him?

I remember little of the journey from Ascot to Huyton except my sorrow at parting from my Hull friends. The vagaries of war are always unpredictable, and rumours had been rife before we left Ascot that our final destination would probably be Canada.

But even if it was true, there was every possibility that we would end up in different camps. I was to meet them again on the boat crossing to the Isle of Man some months later, but now we were heading once again for the Liverpool area. On arrival at Lime Street we changed trains and finally reached the small station of Huyton. We did not know its identity since stations did not carry name boards during the war years. However, Liverpool members told us where we were, and from the station we were to walk to our camp, a mile and a half away. Amusing things happened en route. Some of those with homes in the locality simply stepped on to the footpath and allowed the column to move on to its destination. We saw them do this and naturally said nothing. We knew the fun we were going to have when we arrived at our new camp!

This was very different to Ascot. It was a new housing estate commandeered by the Government for use as a dispersal camp, and we knew we would be there for only a limited time.

It was like all other camps, in that it was surrounded by double barbed wire, with sentry boxes at the entrance. We walked through into the compound and were told to line up for a roll call. This was where the fun started. Some of those at the beginning of a row after being counted would appear at the far end to be counted again. There was always a double check, the second differing from the first, so we were counted yet again. The third differed yet again, and after five counts, all of which were different, the commandant gave up and we were billeted in the houses.

The following morning the roll call showed five persons missing from the required number. Later in the morning a man presented himself at the gate asking to be let in. He had spent the night at home with his very surprised wife, and had to be identified before he was allowed to enter. Later in the day two more appeared asking for admission, and eventually all absentees returned. Why did they do this? Because the only alternative to returning to the camp was to be on the run, and under the circumstances this had little to recommend it, if only because it would create anxiety for one's family.

Liverpool was by now suffering regular bombing raids, many of them in daylight. Frequently between midday and two o'clock bombers would sweep over the camp on their way to city and dock targets. Quite close to the camp were a series of anti-aircraft batteries which hurled a heavy barrage against the intruders, and our houses were peppered with spent ammunition. It was wise to remain under cover at these times.

We never saw any bombers brought down although quite often they appeared to be hit. Numerous detainees volunteered for bomb damage clearance and many did splendid salvagework both in the dock area and other heavily damaged districts.

I was now receiving regular visits from Edith accompanied by parcels of home-baked delicacies. On one occasion I shared some of these with Frank Wiseman who usually acted as compere for our concerts, and production manager on the rare occasions when we attempted a play.

Before his arrest he had been on the senior teaching staff of Worcester Cathedral School, and reminded me of my earlier schoolmaster, Mr. Douthwaite, of St. Albans Church. He was an accomplished pianist with a good baritone voice.

One day we were enjoying one of our post-visit snacks, when we were subjected to an unexpected anti-aircraft barrage, the spent shells raining on the roofs like confetti at a wedding. The barrage appeared to be much heavier than any we had known and there was the possibility that some aircraft might jettison their load before reaching their target. Although the housing estate that was our camp had only been completed in the early months of the war, it was surprising that no air raid shelters had been provided, particularly as the estate was owned by the local council. There was no evidence either of the existence of any cover for the military personnel responsible for the running of the camp, but there might have been some form of underground shelter for their use we could not see.

As my arm was still in plaster there was virtually little work which I could do and although I would have welcomed the opportunity of leaving the camp for a few hours, I was clearly not considered suitable.

After a few weeks at Huyton arrangements were made for me to visit Rainhill Military Hospital for x-rays on my arm in the hope that the fractures would have healed and the plaster could be removed.

The daily pint of milk had not been continued after leaving Ascot, and although I inquired, the camp medical officer expressed no interest, his indifference doing nothing to endear the military authorities to me.

At every turn I was treated to behaviour which contributed to my mounting intransigence towards the guards. I was repeatedly made aware of the thinly-veiled antagonism against us, which as the fortunes of war further turned against Britain, became more and more apparent. It was still some time before the Government realised that as unconvicted civilians we should never have been placed under military control. When this was finally understood, sometime later on the Isle of Man, the Government removed us from military control and placed us under the authority of the Metropolitan Police.

After the x-rays it was decided to remove the plaster, but that I should remain there for a week before returning to the camp. My wife knew where I was and told my father who took advantage of Blackburn's proximity to pay a visit.

He had never condemned me for my political views, but the visit obviously embarrassed him, and there was tension between us which I did not know how to dispel. I think we were both relieved when the time came for him to leave. I did not see him again until years later after the war. There were three other detainees in the hospital at this time, one of them having an ulcerated arm that had failed to heal. His fiancée had been to visit him one day, and with my prior knowledge they planned that he would escape from hospital that night, and join her for a few days of freedom.

Since we were in a small separate ward we were not subject to the usual hospital discipline, and as we could wear pyjamas during the day, it was agreed that he would don my pair until it was fairly dark. He would return my pyjamas which I would put on, strip, and squeeze himself through the small window in the adjoining toilet. We would then pass his clothes to him whereupon he would dress and make his way to his rendezvous with his fiancée. After a terrific struggle he managed to get through the window. We closed it, I donned my pyjamas and got into bed.

We were awakened in the early hours after the night nurse, making her rounds, had found an empty bed in our small ward. The police arrived with tracker dogs, and we were questioned, but of course we knew nothing of his whereabouts. Two dogs were brought into the ward and were taken to his bed to inhale the body smell. When they were unleashed they both came straight to my bed and started to nuzzle me. I was not afraid of dogs and showed no alarm. The police made three attempts to get a lead from the dogs and in each case they came straight to my bed. The police had to withdraw, and I never knew whether they ever suspected collusion. We were moved to the Isle of Man shortly after but I learned that the escapee was picked up about three weeks afterwards in London and had been lodged in Brixton. But by the time I reached there much later, he had been released.

Shortly after our move to Huyton, brother Sydney visited Vic King in the more relaxed atmosphere of York, where he met many old friends. He then accompanied Edith to see me at Huyton, and since it was difficult to tell us apart, it was agreed that he would come again the following Saturday and that during the visit we would exchange roles. Sydney knew many of the members in the camp, and arrangements had been made for him to be met as soon as he came through the gate and taken to the house where I was domiciled. All other inmates in the house had been informed of the plan. I was to return the following week, when the re-exchange would take place, and I would re-enter the camp. The best-laid plans of mice and men gang oft agley, and so did ours!

On the following Wednesday we were moved without warning to the Isle of Man, and when Syd and Edith arrived the following Saturday the camp was empty. If my escape had been planned for a week earlier, Syd would have finished up in the Isle of Man, and it is more than likely that a detention order for him would have been issued by the Home Secretary.

Huyton, as I have explained, was a dispersal camp, and the previous inmates had been a mixed bag of aliens, recent pre-war immigrants and persons of doubtful character. The houses in which we were detained were all semi-detached. There were stories emanating from the military guards that there had been two suicides in the camp, in each case the bodies having been found hanging behind the rear door of the same house. This was now locked and double padlocked, front and rear. Some of us were curious and wanted to see inside, and I was one of a party which decided to break in. I wished afterwards that I had not. It was a most eerie experience. Is it possible to feel a sense of palpable evil in the atmosphere? I believe it is. I could almost smell it, and it became apparent as soon as we closed the rear door which we had forced open. I wanted to turn round and return to the good clean air, but on the other hand I was facing a challenge and had to proceed. We met nothing untoward until we climbed the stairs and entered the bedrooms. The walls of each of which were covered in murals depicting various aspects of sexual aberration.

There was a cock-loft which showed obvious signs of constant use, and we climbed up to see exactly what it had been used for. The cross beams were partially covered to create a rough covered area, and against the chimney breast was what appeared to be the semblance of a crude altar with two black candles. No one had much to say and we did not stay long. We tried to burn the place down but had to be careful that the occupants of the next house were not put at risk. We found an amount of flammable material and set it alight, then informed the neighbours that there was a fire. This was brought under control but not before the house had been extensively damaged. I can only assume that the place had been used for some kind of malevolent form of 'old religion', with black magic undertones. Today the perversion has more adherents than ever. The Prince of Darkness extends His Rule as Christianity loses its hold on the peoples of the West, and morals cease to have any practised value.I do not say that morals have no value, but that they have no practised value. Therein lies the difference.

And so in that spring of 1941, we entrained once more for Lime Street after our mile and a half walk to Huyton Station. I remember forming up on the platform cleared of the general public. But how we got to the Pier Head and boarded the boat for Douglas I do not remember. It was lucky for me that I had not acquired much in the way of belongings, because although I no longer had plaster on my arm, I had been warned only to use it with great care.

Fortunately the sea crossing was mild. The detainees were herded together on the upper deck and although there were many civilian passengers on board, we were not encouraged to converse with them. We were under a military guard who kept themselves in evidence and we were restricted to the upper deck. The crossing was uneventful, and after arrival in Douglas we were lined up on the quayside before boarding coaches. I knew the island well, having spent many holidays there in my early manhood. Soon after we had left Douglas behind we were told that our destination was Peel which again I knew was on the opposite side of the island.

When we arrived I saw that my suspicion that we would be accommodated on the sea front was correct. But this was only one-half of the camp, which was on two levels, one consisting of large boarding houses fronting the sea wall with a secondary row of smaller houses on a higher level with a semi-terraced hillside which was part of the compound separating the two.

Final destination for most British Union detainees was Peveril Camp, Peel, Isle of Man, that had become "the Island of barbed wire". The above photo shows Mooragh Camp.

On the lower level, extending beyond the houses was a tennis court and what had once been a small cafe and shop. This became the camp tuck-shop from which we could make limited purchases using special paper money issued by camp officials against one's credit resources. There was a variety of work in the camp, all of which earned credits to a maximum of three shillings a week. House cleaners, cooks, camp hygiene attendants, and other outdoor work on local farms all received the same level of payment.

Initially we were allowed to choose our house-sharing companion, but once the decision was made a change to another house required official approval. I opted for one of the larger houses on the higher level where it was agreed I would be cook. We drew our daily raw rations from the quartermaster and each house was responsible for the preparation of meals for the number living there. It was according to the size of the house and the number of residents whether it was necessary for an assistant cook. We qualified.

During my initial stay in the camp I remained in the same house, number twenty-five. The name of my assistant is worth recording. He was of Anglo-German parentage and prior to the First World War, his father had been the largest landowner in Europe, much of his property being sequestered to the newly re-created country of Poland when the Poles seized most of Silesia. His mother, Daisy Cornwallis-West, was English, and much of his youth and early manhood had been spent in England. He spoke English without any trace of accent. His name — His Highness, The Prince of Pless, John Henry to his friends. He was released during my absence from the camp and joined the army as a private. I did not see him after the war. We always worked very amicably together. In 1984, he and his brother died within a week of one another.

The food was to say the least meagre, with a meat ration of minute proportions issued three times a week. Other days it was fish, and this was sometimes herrings in brine which had been pickled during World War I and was very unpalatable unless carefully treated and camouflaged, first by overnight soaking to extract the excessive salt and then casseroled with spices and herbs. Even so it was not a popular dish.

If some of the house occupants were farm workers, rabbits and sometimes a hare would be brought in to supplement the normal fare. During the mackerel season we often would be issued with fresh fish and these were easy to gut and bone out. They made a delicious change when soused in malt vinegar.

There was a different atmosphere in Peveril Camp — its official title — to any we had previously experienced. It was as if subconsciously we realised that this was our last move and that in all probability we should remain here until released. This engendered a different outlook in general and the majority of us became resigned to our fate. Releases were occurring almost every week, sometimes singly, sometimes in batches of four or six. These could occur even without a secondary hearing as a result of pressure on the Home Secretary from the detainee's M.P. who might have been badgered by a wife or family.

I know that on two occasions my wife wrote to the Member for our constituency, North-West Hull. Although his efforts on my behalf were not successful, he at least tried, and wrote to my wife informing her of his attempts. We never knew from one day to another when we were likely to be released and this contributed to a fatalistic attitude.

Life was also more tolerable here and an attitude of permanency created a more placid outlook, though not for everyone. There were some who still bitterly resented internment, though at the time I was not one of them. Subsequent behaviour on the part of one man was to reactivate my dormant feelings with unexpected results, however, and it was while at Peel that I began to subconsciously categorise the inmates. We had Anglo-Germans, Anglo-Italians, British Union members, active and non-active, members of the Link and the Anglo-German Fellowship, associates of the Hamburg-based Deutschefichtebund, and finally special groups of people some of whom were not even of British nationality, but who had been detained soon after the outbreak of war.

Their arrests were on direct recommendations from MI5 and MI6. There were quite a number in this category not all of whom I remember by name. Quentin Joyce was the youngest brother of William, Lord Haw-Haw — his other brother, Frank, had been a member of the B.U.F.; Professor Darwin-Fox was an intellectual who appeared to have had fingers in many international pies: Harry St. John Philby was the famous explorer and father of the notorious Kim, who had, for many years, been a close confident of Ibn Saud during his early tribal campaigning in Arabia that finally resulted in the establishment of the Saud dynasty of today; Admiral Niki Wolkoff of the Imperial Russian Navy, whose daughter, Anna, had been convicted of treason in 1940 and jailed for 10 years for her part in the Tyler Kent case.

Kent, a cipher clerk in the United States Embassy in London, had supplied copies of correspondence between Churchill and Roosevelt taken from Embassy files, to Anna Wolkoff. These reached Captain Ramsey, the Conservative MP for Peebles, and founder of the "Right Club". It was hinted that Ramsey had laid information before the King, which had it been made public, would have been greatly embarrassing for a senior member of the Government. In any event Ramsey was detained under 18b. It should be made clear that no British Union supporter was involved in this affair. He never volunteered any explanation for these events, and Mosley thought him very foolish not to have told the whole story in the House of Commons. Kent, meantime, had been convicted and imprisoned in the Tower of London, and later on his eventual release, surreptitiously deported to the United States. What a story he could tell, but his lips remained sealed.

There was one man whose name I will not disclose. I recently supplied what background recollections I had to his daughter. She had been making inquiries about her father's detention while in England on holiday from Canada. He was a Canadian journalist and in the early months of the war was on assignment to the American magazine, Time.

I believe he knew a great deal, still unpublished, of the Tyler Kent-Anna Wolkoff story, and his detention was the result of official fears that he might splash the story in the American press to the mutual embarrassment of the British and American governments. He remained very secretive throughout the whole period of his detention, and after the war until death, even within his own family.

Captain Elwin Wright was another mysterious individual. He

claimed to be a practising psychiatrist and that through his psychiatric couch had become privy to information of a sensational nature. He 'joined' British Union whilst detained, and was secretary of the Anglo-German Fellowship. He was extremely knowledgeable particularly in the continental geopolitical field. He was very pro-German but not in any way anti-Semitic.

Even in the early days he was not convinced of ultimate German victory. He thought a reversal of military trends more than possible and forecast that if Germany lost, communism would become the ruling power throughout that land. History has proved him half right.

The black-bearded Doctor Jellic was probably the most fascinating individual in the whole camp, certainly the most intriguing person I met during my entire period of detention. He was a highly nationalistic Croatian who did not acknowledge the sovereignty of the Yugoslavian monarchy over his country. I heard him claim to have been involved in the assassination of King Alexander of Yugoslavia in Marseilles while on an official State Visit to France, and later been an active supporter of Hitler from the time of the abortive Munich Putsch. Early in 1940 he was to visit America to propagate Germany's cause and thereby assist in preventing the entry of America into the war.

In furtherance of this objective, he booked passage on an Italian ship, but he did not succeed in reaching America. At the time Italy had not entered the conflict, and although a partner in the Axis was still neutral.

British secret sources knew of Jellic's moves, and were also aware of his presence as a passenger on this Italian ship. Shortly after leaving the Mediterranean for the Atlantic a Royal Naval vessel commanded the neutral Italian ship to stop engines, sent a party aboard and Jellic was forcibly removed. Needless to say, this breach of International Law was not publicised, nor was our occupancy of Iceland against the wishes of the Icelandic peoples to remain neutral. Jellic was first taken to Gibraltar and then brought to England in company with a number of pro-Franco Gibraltarians, many of whom I later met at Ascot camp. He spoke excellent English and was a captivating raconteur. His knowledge of internal European politics and double-dealing chicanery could have formed the basis of many a post-war spy story.

He could have made a fortune from his memoirs but they would have had to be written as fiction. No publisher would surely have dared publish them as an accurate history of central Europe and machinations during the inter-war years. Jellic remained in London for a number of years after the war and then he faded from view, returning perhaps to the murky world of central European intrigue.

Reverting to the more conventional type of detainee, I often think of Chris Schirmer, and not surprisingly perhaps, since he executed two paintings of me. He was also of mixed parentage, but should not have been in our camp since he had an English mother, had been born in Cork and should therefore have been classed as an alien.

Chris was on a work permit at the outbreak of war as a salesman for Agfa films and he told me that since he had an Irish passport, he had been overlooked in the early round-up. He had a natural flair for painting landscapes but was also a quite creditable portrait painter.

In July 1984, a book was published entitled 'Island of Barbed Wire' by Connery Chappel which included details of an escape from Peel camp during our stay there. It implied that all the internees at Peel were in the same camp. This, of course, was not so. There were, as I have mentioned, two camps but they were well separated and the inmates of each never came into contact.

An article in the Isle of Man Courier referring to the escape, suggests that Nikolaus Pevsner, Lord Weidenfeld, Charles Forte, Geoffrey Elton and Tiny Rowland were all in the same camp, and that there were fights between Jews and Fascists. This is untrue. We did have a Geoffrey Elton and more than one Rowland in our camp, one a Blackshirt, and the other, the young Tiny Rowland of later financial fame, who was with us for but a short period.

In my recollection there were three escapes, one of whom was reputed to be an I.R.A. man. The other two were members of British Union, Arthur Mason, from East London, Joseph Barry and Joseph Walker. Arthur, former Limehouse District Leader, now lives in Adelaide, and I contacted him while I was in Australia in 1984.

The house from which they escaped was unoccupied, the conspirators all living in the adjoining house. It was because the house was vacant and supposedly locked up that they were able to dig the tunnel without being observed. A large proportion of the floor boards of his house were used for shoring up the roof of the tunnel. Lighting, supplied from the house in which they lived, presented no problems since electricity usage in the camp was never checked for consumption.

It was natural that the Irish, where possible, would choose to live together. I think their house was numbered 13, and I knew to some extent of their intention to escape. One of them had already been over the wire at least once when we were in Huyton, and after visiting his family in the Liverpool area, returned to the camp of his own volition the following day. On this occasion we were tipped off that the escape had been made, and we covered the roll call by returning to the house after the count, reappearing at the house from which the numbers would be short.

Neither the escort nor the officer of the day knew every inmate of every house and was therefore unable to suspect that a switch had been made. By this means we covered the escape for a full day. To make deception easier, releases and transfers were taking place regularly so that the requisite number of detainees was always changing.

The house in which I lived had a cellar and I calculated that all the houses in the row had them too. I also assumed that the escape tunnel was dug through the cellar wall facing the barbed wire perimeter, but this was not so. The entrance to the tunnel was at the foot of a deep pit, the earth disposed of by one of the inmates officially employed inside the camp as a gardener-cum-camp labourer.

The escapees were hoping to reach Ireland but were picked up after being sighted by a spotter plane only a few miles off the Irish coast. They were brought back to the camp in the late afternoon of the second day, and after a tumultuous welcome by the detainees, were taken straight to the guardhouse.

The welcome which they received angered Captain Ryan who was deputising for the Commandant who was away on leave.

He was very unpopular with the detainees and obviously viewed us with great distaste. His resultant behaviour ought not to have surprised us, but my immediate reaction was one of deep anger. I was the first to be made aware of his attitude to the escapees, and it would probably be fair to say that as a result I was mainly responsible for what followed.

When anyone was in the guardhouse it was the custom that all main meals would be provided from inside the camp. Once prepared, it would be taken to the main gate where an escort would be requested, and then taken under escort to the guardhouse. There was no reason to suppose that normal procedure would not apply in this case.

I had always been very friendly with the Irish boys, having known them from my early days in the Movement, and I was not surprised when I was asked by another occupant of the house, from which they had escaped, to provide a hot meal for them. When it was ready I took it down from my kitchen to the main gate where I asked for an escort to the guardhouse. After a 'phone call through to the administrative headquarters the request was refused. Since this was contrary to procedure I asked again, and after another 'phone call, permission for an escort was once more refused.

I took the meal back to the kitchen and reported the incident to the camp leader Mick Clarke who found my story difficult to believe since it was contrary to agreed practice. He came with me to the kitchen, where I again collected the meal, and accompanied me to the main gate. This time he requested an escort for a prepared meal to be taken to the guardhouse. After yet another 'phone call it was again refused. The camp leader then asked in his official capacity upon whose authority the refusal had been made, and the reason for refusal.

The reply came back that the decision had been made by the Acting Commandant, who had decided that since the escapees had been without a hot meal for over two days it would not harm them to go without for three days. At this I 'blew my top', and stormed away from the gate in a very angry frame of mind.

It was coincidental that at the time Edith and the children were visiting me during a holiday from her work place in Southport, and were staying in Peel. They had been to see me the afternoon that the escapees were returned to detention. Naturally I explained to my wife what had taken place the previous day in the camp and at the time when we were not aware of their recapture.

Ryan's action provoked a spontaneous outburst of resentment, which resulted in a demonstration at the main gate demanding a change of heart. Ryan remained adamant, and as a result a full-scale riot developed, involving practically the entire camp, and forcing the retreat of the guards from the main gate under a hail of missiles. It was probably my justifiable anger which sparked off the riotous assembly which followed, since my telling of the circumstances lost nothing in the recounting of the story.

The camp area was roughly rectangular with a row of houses on the sea front. Where they began a side road climbed a slight rise and then bore to the left where a second row of houses formed the higher level of accommodation. The perimeter of barbed wire surrounding the camp ran down the centre of the road, completely surrounding the camp compound.

At the base of the hill and outside the perimeter was the Creg Malin Hotel, a fairly large building with outhouses. The hotel was the administrative offices for the military and its outhouses were used for minor administrative purposes and included a large room for visitors.

Whenever the military attempted to enter the camp in a bid to restore order, they were met with a hail of missiles. The garden walls of the lower houses were torn down and hurled against the main gate and the hotel itself, most of whose windows abutting the side road were smashed as a result.

The riot lasted throughout the night, and was so noisy that Edith and the children, staying in Peel, could not sleep. They were naturally deeply concerned as to the cause of the disturbance, but no civilian was allowed to approach the camp.

Appeals by the military for a cessation of hostilities were met with the demand that I should be allowed to take a meal to the guardhouse, but Ryan consistently refused to give way. So did we. Eventually reporters arrived and were provided with seats at the upper window of the hotel. We countered with jets of water from fire hoses attached to the house taps abutting the road. Many press men were thoroughly drenched to our great delight, for they were no friends of ours. Some thrust cameras through the windows to photograph events for the newsreel programmes, but I understand that the films were never shown. Perhaps the Government did not wish its inability to maintain authority to be made public. The following morning there was no roll call since we would not allow any member of the military to enter the camp. We made it quite evident that although we were without rations, we were in control.

Later that day the Commandant hurriedly returned in an effort to restore peace. But we were not in a conciliatory mood, nor would we agree that a deputation leave the camp to talk with him. We suspected that if we did, the members of the delegation might also end up in the guardhouse.

The authorities were afraid that we might attempt a mass break-out, though had we done so there was little that we could have achieved, except to rampage through the town and we had no quarrel with the local people — with the exception of the proprietor of the Creg Malin Hotel, who was bitterly hostile to us. The final result was that the Home Secretary's Parliamentary Private Secretary, Osbert Peake, was flown by special 'plane to the island and requested permission to enter the camp. This was not made public then or since. We agreed on condition that he gave an assurance that no punitive action be taken against anyone regarded as a ringleader. This assurance Osbert Peake gave in the name of the Government. Some of us were to learn later what that assurance was worth : virtually nothing.

Peake came into the camp accompanied, as we had requested, by the commandant. He was obviously afraid but did his best not to show it, for which I gave him credit. He might even have been sincere when he gave us his assurance of no retribution, but Herbert Morrison, like Brutus 'Was not an Honourable man'. We never forgot that our jailor had been a conscientious objector during World War 1.

Mick Clarke explained the circumstances which had led up to the riot, and requested Ryan's removal from the camp. Peake could not guarantee this, but promised that the whole question of who should be responsible for overall control of the camp would be looked into. We then agreed to lift our ban against entry by members of the military and they, in turn, agreed that there would be no further refusal to allow food to inmates of the guardhouses. The commandant admitted that Ryan had been at fault in his initial refusal.

The disturbance ended immediately, and life in the camp returned to normal and the following afternoon I received another visit from Edith and the children who later returned to the mainland. I was to see them again in Walton Gaol, to their surprise and mine.

It was later reported that the wire perimeter was electrified and that the power was actually switched on during the disturbance. I do not know if this was true but as the bricks made contact with the wire there were occasional sparks. If there had been any electrification I think we should have been informed, but I have no proof that this was the case.

Mick Clarke was a nationally known figure in British Union, a very forceful and dynamic speaker. He came into prominence in East London, and was extremely popular with the members. For a number of years he had been on the paid staff of the Movement and had originally been held in Brixton with other leading figures, some of whom remained there until their release.

We were surprised when shortly after our arrival in Peel Mick joined us. I noticed a great change in his personality. He was much quieter in his manner and adopted a more equable profile. He was appointed camp leader shortly after his arrival.

We were later told that Ryan was to be transferred to the mainland and there was some expression of delight at what appeared to be an act of appeasement by the authorities. We should have known better. British governments of the era were never magnanimous towards those in their power. Then came the day that Ryan left the camp. It had been raining heavily and the paths on the grassy terraces were very muddy. Ryan was making his final inspection and after touring the houses on the higher level made his way back to the main gate when he lost his footing. There was already a chorus of cheering detainees who were witnessing his approaching departure, and to our great delight he slipped and rolled down the muddy hillside. He picked himself up, and although in a very muddy condition, walked the remaining distance to the gate with more dignity than I would have thought him capable of.

When, a few weeks later, I was told on morning roll call to pack my bags and report to the gate I thought that I was going home.

But arriving at the gate I found I was not alone. There were 18 of us, including Mick Clarke, and other camp representatives who had met and talked with the Commandant and Osbert Peake. By the time we passed through the gate and into the Creg Malin Hotel, our feelings were somewhat despondent.

I do not, now, remember all the names of our party. There was Charlie Hammond, a man named Hill, a Welshman called Jimmy who had been in the Army for many months and had even been evacuated from Dunkirk only to be interned on his return, a Manchester member called Lomax, an epileptic

Italian Pasquale de Macio, another Welshman, Ashworth-Jones, myself and four others. We were informed that we were being returned to the mainland but not told of our destination, nor the reason for our removal from Peel. By this time the entire camp knew of the unusual circumstances of our departure, since they were now without a camp leader.

For some hours we were kept under close surveillance. After a meal we were taken outside into a large yard at the back of the hotel. We were immediately surrounded by a double row of soldiers armed with rifles and fixed bayonets, with the officer in charge carrying a revolver which he made no attempt to conceal. Inside this military ring was a large furniture van with the large rear drop door open, and on the outside, two bren gun carriers fully armed and complete with army personnel to operate them. We were ordered into the van and once inside the door was closed and battened with some form of cross bolt.

The vehicle started to move. We were, of course, in complete darkness and had the situation not been so farcical might have felt a little frightened. I was told later, by an eye witness that when the party moved off it was headed by a bren gun carrier complete with gunner and officer, followed by an army transport vehicle with half the contingent of soldiers, the furniture van, then another army transport vehicle carrying the remaining solders with the rear brought up by another bren gun carrier, again with gunner and officer.

We travelled at a fairly rapid pace, and since there was no seating, were thrown about in the darkened van. About an hour later the vehicle stopped and after a short delay and some undistinguishable conversation we moved on, but soon stopped again.

There was the sound of much rapid movement outside and the muted shout of orders. Then the door of the van was opened and we were ordered out. I was transported back in time to Ruritania and to the film set of "The Prisoner of Zenda'. Any moment now Ronald Colman, in his character of Rudolph Rassendyl, would surely appear.

We found ourselves in a large cobbled stone enclosure, surrounded once more by soldiers, this time with rifles raised to the shoulder in firing position and an officer now brandishing a revolver. We had reached the depths of absurdity. Had we shown any hostility and the officer had ordered his men to fire, they would have opened up not only at us but at their own men on the opposite side of the circle. It was positively ludicrous. Far from being intimidated we were highly amused and showed it. Our obvious derogatory attitude somewhat displeased the officer, but there was little that he could do.

We were then addressed by a smartly attired civilian who told us that we had arrived at Douglas Gaol where we were to spend the night before being returned to the mainland. He was quite civil, and assured us that he would not make our overnight stay too uncomfortable. To be spoken to in civil tones was something to which we had become unaccustomed.

We were divided into four parties with three allocated to cells much larger than I had known in Walton. The floors were wooden and polished. There were no beds but we were provided with comfortable palliasses, pillows and sheets and given an evening meal which I remember was quite palatable. Concern as to our ultimate future rather inhibited restful sleep but morning eventually came and we were served the usual prison breakfast. We were then reloaded into the van and the previous day's procession reformed, but this time with a little light allowed in.

However, we were unprepared for the civilian reception that greeted our arrival at the dockside. There were boos and cat-calls as we walked towards the boat. From the moment of boarding we were kept under close guard and restricted to a specially roped-off section of the upper deck with the army present in great numbers. There were also a small number of London policemen who would be responsible for us once we docked on the Lancashire Coast.

When we arrived at Fleetwood the dockside was cleared of ordinary passengers before we were allowed off, although at least one press photographer was there using his camera.

Boarding a train we were told we were going to Walton which I received with mixed feelings. I knew it meant that I would receive regular visits from Edith, but from experience I knew that Walton was the worst of our jails. Little time was wasted in reception and we were soon moved into the prison proper. Liverpool had been subjected to much heavy bombing and the prison had been severely damaged. We were placed in isolation in an unused wing which had suffered from the aerial raids. The roof was missing and sections of the fourth and fifth landings had been badly hit. When it rained the basement was flooded but we were placed in cells on the first landing. It was now late November and already beginning to get quite cold, but there was no heating except a coal fire in the office of the prison staff, a double-sized cell on the corner abutting the centre from which the other wings fanned out like spokes in a wheel.

There had been a change of governor since our early days and the present title holder was not as sadistic as his predecessor. We were not ordered to see him, instead he came to us. He told us our cell doors would remain open from six in the morning until ten at night and we would be given the normal prison fare. However, we could supplement this by parcels brought or sent in, or by using our own financial resources, if either of the prison officers permanently on duty were willing to make purchases on our behalf.

Books from the prison library were available to us and we could have any type of game that was adaptable for use either in the wing or in the exercise area outside. Weekly visits were not restricted to the normal twenty minutes, but extended within reasonable limits. Two outgoing letters instead of the usual one, and no limit on incoming mail.

The two officers on duty interchanged with two others so that we were always under the same authoritative control. They were all reasonable men, not to be compared in any way with those we had known previously in Walton, and although not actually friendly, they were at least co-operative and not openly antagonistic. Life, it appeared, would be bearable, but what of the guarantee that Osbert Peake had given to us at Peel that there would be no reprisals?

My wife was made aware of my re-arrival in Walton even before I had time to write to her. A copy of the News Chronicle containing my photograph arriving at Fleetwood was thrown at her when she was at breakfast in the canteen of the bakery where she worked. The accompanying comment was, "That's your bloody husband, isn't it? He's still causing trouble, even after being locked up".

I had worked with this gallant soul when I had first gone to Southport in 1927, and he was now my wife's foreman. This photograph in the paper did not make life any easier for Edith.

Life during this second Walton spell was very uneventful, though there was a little coming and going in our numbers. By now all detainees had been to a tribunal hearing and after a lapse of six months were entitled to ask for another. From our original number of eighteen, we had been reduced, by the end of January of 1942, to eleven. One of the first to be moved on was Mick Clarke. I was to see him only twice more, first in London and then in Manchester, after the war.

I now heard that I was to be transferred to Brixton, which could mean that I was to have a second tribunal hearing. I was not too optimistic about my chances of release, but at least I would try not to be deliberately aggressive in any answers although I was still unwilling to compromise my opposition to the war and my determination to remain true to my principles. Although prepared to give a guarantee that I would refrain from politics and public expression of my views, this was the limit to which I was prepared to go.

I sent a telegram to Edith telling her of my move, and travelled to London by train accompanied by prison officers. On arrival in Brixton I met up with some officers of the movement whom I had not seen since April 1940, among them Hector McKecknie, Captain Donovan and Francis-Hawkins. Both Donovan and Francis-Hawkins were much quieter than I had previously known them to be but McKecknie was his usual ebullient self.

On my second Saturday there, I was told I had a visitor. I asked if there had been a mistake because I could think of no-one likely to visit me. I was assured there was no mistake and I hurried to the visiting reception area. Shown into the usual screened partition cubicle I was surprised to see Edith's eldest sister Nellie who lived in Sussex. She had spent quite some time with us in Hull just prior to and after the birth of my son in January 1940, and we were very good friends. She had never expressed any objections to my politics. I have always been grateful for the visits she paid me during my three month stay in Brixton. Bless you, Nellie.

I cannot recall the name of the chairman at my second hearing, and in fact I remember very little about it. The hearing lasted a very short period, and I got the impression that it was arranged only because of pressures on the Home Secretary, and that a decision to keep me under detention had already been made. It was so casual throughout that little effort was made to discover if there had been any change in my attitude. To maintain the charade of a fair hearing I was kept waiting quite some time for a decision, but I had warned my wife not to be optimistic. By the time I arrived in Brixton, Oswald Mosley had been transferred to Holloway together with Major de Laessoe where they joined their wives in detention. I missed him by a few weeks. Other than that there were more detainees in Brixton than in Walton and there was little to choose between the conditions in the two prisons.

About this time there was an attempt by a detainee to commit suicide. He cut both wrists but was found in time for his life to be saved. Shortly after he was released. Then came notice of the decision of the Home Secretary not to release me, and not long after I was told I would be returning to Walton. When I arrived back our numbers had been reduced to eight. Then one day, without prior warning, we were told to collect our belongings — we were going back to the Isle of Man. Fortunately I was able to let my wife know before we left.

After my earlier experience in Walton, I never thought I would have a good word to say about any prison warder, but I must, in fairness, say that the treatment we received during our second period was far better. There was no suggestion of any return to the wretched conditions that greeted us in June 1940.

Whether this was the result of directives from above or because there had been a lessening of general antagonisms towards us I did not even try to find out. I was just satisfied to enjoy, if that's the word, our improved lot.

Unfortunately, however, the repetition of prison fare had resulted in a worsening of my bowel condition and constipation with an accompanying irritation of the anus which scant medical attention did little to improve.

The journey to the Isle of Man was uneventful and again the weather was quite mild. Our return to the camp must have been notified either officially or by grapevine since we were given quite a welcome. On our arrival at the Creg Malin Hotel we were interviewed separately by an Inspector Munt, who said that I had been stigmatised as a troublemaker and he hoped I would not give him any cause for concern. My hackles immediately began to rise but noticing this he asked me to be calm and promised he would listen to what I had to say. I told him that I had never looked upon myself as a troublemaker but that I did perhaps react too quickly to what I thought were injustices.

I said that my willingness to register for national service had been dependent on my release, and that I could scarcely be expected to enlist to fight in a "War for Freedom", at a time when my own freedom was being denied me. This was a travesty of justice, and would have been entirely hypocritical for me to connive in it.

I referred to my stay in Ascot, where there had never been any suggestion of non co-operation. The same could also be said of my stay in Huyton. I then briefly explained the background to the disturbances in Peel prior to my removal, pointing out that it was Captain Ryan who had acted in an unreasonable manner, hence his subsequent removal from the camp. I also pointed out that throughout my time in Liverpool and Brixton, during my enforced absence from the camp, there had never been any suggestion that I had caused trouble.

Inspector Munt listened carefully but made no comment. So far as he was concerned, I was starting with a clean sheet and I would be judged on my general behaviour. He asked if I intended to work in the camp and I said that I hoped to again become a house cook. To this he made no comment. His attitude was authoritative but almost friendly, and I felt reassured. I did not speak to him again, however, until the morning of my release, almost eighteen months later.

Our armed forces continued to suffer reverses in North Africa and Burma, as well as losses at sea, and the general atmosphere was hardly conductive to a build-up of releases, although these continued. I began to feel I could expect no change in my own fortunes, and almost subconsciously became resigned to a continuance of my detention for an indeterminate period.

I discovered on my return that two more of my Hull members had been detained, Eric Haldenby and Arthur Marson. After a short stay in Brixton they arrived at Peel, and in each case were released after a brief detention only to be re-arrested after a short period of freedom. They were finally released in 1944 and

I never saw Eric again. I heard he had moved down South where he had found himself a job. Arthur returned to Hull for some years and we had a 'reunion' when I visited him there around 1950 and learned that he had been re-arrested for not keeping the conditions of his earlier release. He went to live abroad shortly after and I lost touch but in 1986 I heard, through the Friends of O.M., an association of old members set up after the death of Mosley, that he had made contact from Germany where he had finally settled and it gave me great joy to telephone him one evening and bring us up to date on our personal experiences of the last 30 years.

Shortly after my return to Peel and his second tribunal hearing Vic King was released. By this time Herbert Morrison had a more malleable attitude towards release recommendations. We had been assured that in many cases recommendations for release had not been acted upon by the Home Secretary, and perhaps parliamentary pressure was being brought upon him to be more conciliatory. There had certainly been an increase in House of Commons questions regarding detainees, particularly those held under Section 18b, la, the section dealing with political prisoners.

It should be stressed that after the official scrutiny of all the letters and files collected from the British Union offices and from the homes of the hundreds of British Union members, and after the most searching hearings and question and answer sessions by leading members of the Bar, not one British Union member was ever brought to trial or charged with an infringement of the law. This alone was clear indication that our arrest was entirely without justification.

Churchill's government of the war and post-war periods never admitted the injustice of their actions, a contemptible omission on the part of a man who's "Passion" for "Freedom" owes more to his purple prose and stage-manager legend than to the cold reality.

By now I had become very efficient at making the best possible use of our limited supplies. I could make pastry when fats became available from outside supplies, farm workers or food parcels from the mainland, and since this was a part of my normal occupation my efforts were better than camp average.

We had our tuck shop from which limited supplies of various commodities could be bought, and were by now receiving our civilian allocation rationing points, in addition to basic rations which we drew from the camp stores.

I started to make simple cakes and pastries from my own supply of purchased ingredients and sold these to the operator of the canteen who in turn retailed them to the general camp inmates. We were supplied with paper money similar to that used in "Monopoly", and this was general camp currency. There was also a certain amount of genuine currency in the camp, which we could receive either by bank transfer to the banking office in the Creg Malin Hotel or passed over at visits.

The camp money was paid out for internal services rendered by cooks, cleaners, gardeners and such like and all outgoing farm workers were credited with the same amount as camp workers. This amounted to three shillings and sixpence per week. I would also make special cakes for celebratory occasions for which I would receive additional payment. I built up quite a good business all of which was perfectly legitimate.

There were three laundries in the camp for those inmates who had neither the will or the ability to do their own washing. We also had two tailors who made new suits and garments as well as carrying out repairs. The customer would provide the material which could be ordered from outside the camp through the camp administration, the personal account being debited on a signed requisition advice note. I had a suit made in the camp which I paid for out of my earnings, and two pairs of corduroy trousers sent from a London firm who supplied a catalogue to the camp.

We even had our own dental mechanic who could either supply new artificial plates or carry out repairs. We also had our own dentist and two doctors, but they acted in concert with the authorities. With additional cooking duties, I was now in receipt of two pounds and seven shillings a week on top of which I probably made another ten shillings a week from my baking efforts. These earnings enabled me to subsidise holidays for my family. I also bought a gold wrist watch and bracelet for Edith.

During this latter part of my stay in Peel I made a couple of attempts to learn German, but with only moderate success. During my schooldays I could absorb knowledge and memorise detail on a wide variety of subjects with comparative ease, but this facility seemed to have deserted me. I did, however, retain a sufficient grounding to enable me to prepare a couple of short addresses in German which I put to use some years later when responding to an official welcome to a visiting trade delegation in the Rathaus in Frankfurt, and again later in Dusseldorf.

I spent most of my spare time during the day reading, and my fare was mixed. Fiction interspersed with economics and philosophy, but of the latter not a great deal. I am too much of an activist to have much time for the more involved intellectual pursuits and I admit that this is one of the weaknesses of my character.

My evenings were invariably taken up with card playing. For close on eighteen months I sat in at a solo school and until a release required a replacement the players were always the same. No wonder I became a good player, and still am today though the sessions are now infrequent. Our original school comprised Ray Guager, a London plumber (whose skills were often in demand); T.J. Ashworth-Jones, the Welshman who was with me on our second sojourn in Walton, and another Welshman whose name escapes me and who on release was replaced by Peter Parker.

Ashworth-Jones was something of a loner, and apart from his passion for the game solo, was always to be found on his own wandering around the compound in all weathers and in all seasons. He had a pitched, penetrating voice and would often call out the psalm singing phrases of the more outlandish religious sects. Two of his favourites were 'God is Love', and 'Hallelujah, Praise The Lord', but one never knew if they were expressions of piety or cynicism. I always suspected they were the latter, but with Ashworth-Jones it did not pay to be too curious or questioning.

He was a great stickler for the rules of the game, and deeply resented any misdeal, because in his school the cards were only shuffled once and that was at the start of the game. No matter how long the session lasted the cards were never reshuffled until the following night. The finest player it was my joy to play with, however, was Ray Gauger. He once called 'Abundance Declared' on a full-suited hand, and as all solo players will know, to take all thirteen tricks on a full-suited hand is almost impossible. We were so taken aback at the success of the hand that we collected our own cards and replayed the game in an attempt to beat the call but without avail. We always played for nominal stakes, so that no one was ever heavily out of pocket.

In the front lounge of House 2 Chris Schirmer had painted murals reminiscent of his beloved Bavaria. They covered the entire wall and were still on the wall many years later when I visited the Isle of Man for a National Chamber of Trade.

I saw to it that the inmates of houses 1 and 2 got, not only the best food available but also what bodily comfort my ingenuity was able to provide. Additional food was provided by relatives and outside workers. There was a rule which applied in most houses, irrespective of reasons for detention, that all food parcels were deposited in the kitchen for the general use of the cook. The result was that those who received few parcels, and there were many, did not feel missed out and consequently there was always a splendid spirit of genuine comradeship among all the detainees. Throughout the entire period of my imprisonment

I never experienced a single instance of animosity or rivalry.

I excelled myself in the preparation of the Christmas dinner for 1942. With supplies from outside via food parcels and purchases plus supplies from outside workers, I provided roast chicken (of indeterminate age!), roast hare and roast rabbit, Christmas pudding and white sauce, with freshly baked hot mince pies to follow. I even made a Christmas cake and decorated it for the evening meal.

In the summer of 1942 I received an unexpected visitor, my brother Sydney. In the early part of the war he had been in the merchant marines on coaster tramps between Hull, London and intervening ports. These were mainly the areas subject to magnetic and other modern types of mining by the enemy. He told me he had left the merchant marine and was now working as a baker in London. This was a reserved occupation and there was a shortage of bakers in London owing to the now heavy and consistent bombing. Many bakers had been killed, no doubt because nearly all bread baking was done at night, the time that most of the raids took place.

It was good to see him again. We hadn't met since the previous summer when our planned exchange had been aborted due to our unexpected move to Peel.

He thought that it was only by volunteering for coastal shipping, followed by his present bread-making commitment in London, that he had been protected from detention. I was inclined to agree with him, but I did not then, nor have I ever since, felt any sense of resentment that of the four Blackshirt brothers I was the only one to be detained. Perhaps my ego subconsciously revelled in it."

By now we were allowed to have film shows in the camp including newsreels with censorship existing in the form of an official list. Among the Mosley detainees were two former cinema owners, who may have been instrumental in getting this concession from the authorities.

It has to be conceded that there was a greater measure of understanding and co-operation now that the military had been replaced by the Metropolitan Police. The early military career of Mosley and some one-third of those detained, may to some extent have been responsible for the almost universal feeling of antagonism between his supporters and their gaolers. There were some exceptions, noticeably the commandant at Ascot, who on one occasion even apologised to us for being our gaoler. He said his task humiliated him.

On the other hand, at Brixton where Mosley and those of his followers whom the authorities thought had status in the Movement, and many were ex-servicemen — every medal given for gallantry in the British Army, except the V.C., being worn in the prison yard — were always well treated. The prison staff there were mostly ex-servicemen — one warder had been a sergeant in Mosley's regiment — and "on the whole were a fine lot" according to Mosley writing in his autobiography "My Life".

There were three occasions when we were allowed the use of a large hall in Peel for a concert and for the presentation of two Edgar Wallace plays. On each occasion Frank Wiseman was compere and producer. The quality of performance was of an exceptionally high standard. We already had a camp band and two concert pianists, and the rendering of some of the more popular classics seemed to me to be exceptional. One of the Anglo-Germans performed a violin concerto, the playing of which remains with me to this day.

Of the Edgar Wallace plays, what shall I say? They were 'The Man Who Knew Too Much', and 'The Man Who Changed His Name'. I played the lead in the latter and a bit part in the former. I know that I quite enjoyed it, and to my surprise, in view of my inability to learn German, I was word perfect, and it was quite a large part with some long scenes. I still have the blanks and imitation revolver that I used in the play.

Edith visited me in the late summer of 1942, this time staying in Douglas making it more of a holiday than on previous visits. Apart from the reality of detention, there was little about which to raise serious objection, and I was happy for her to find some relaxation from the arduous tensions of her daily grind.

I have not attempted to stress or even to express the pressures which were placed upon the wives of detainees, so casually withdrawn from the normal stream of civilian life. To have to work in the outside world among a workforce which looked upon your husband as a potential or actual traitor required character of exceptional quality. Most wives of husbands of military age had to face the permanent hazard of the normal casualties of war time, but they did not have to contend with the daily snide comment that the fifth column husband was not facing the hazards of warfare, but was skulking in the holiday resort of The Isle of Man and dodging his patriotic duty.

Political detainees like myself, at least had the consolation of a belief, a commitment to an ideal, that sustained the spirit, enabling it to survive even in the tumultuous atmosphere of war. But the wife of the detainee — what commitment or belief had she to help her to survive the daily harassment of an uncharitable circle of neighbours and workmates?

When I was arrested Edith was deprived of her only source of income, my weekly wage. She was virtually destitute and when she asked for temporary help from the Southport offices of the Public Assistance Board was met with abuse. She was asked about the whereabouts of her husband and her resultant need, and upon stating that her husband was in prison on a Detention Order, this kind and charitable freedom-loving example of Enlightened England told her that her husband was "a traitor and

Photo of wife Edith, daughter Rose, and 6 month old Cedric taken shortly after author's arrest.

a fifth columnist who ought to be shot, that there was no help forthcoming for her, and that as far as he was concerned she and her children could starve".

I doubt if anyone has ever attempted to write of the sufferings of the families of the detainees; the humiliations, the oft-spoken abuse, and the more often unspoken discriminatory treatment, the loneliness and the disappearance of fair-weather friends, the disapproval of relatives and the comments condemning the absent husband, and even the cruelty of school children who would taunt the child or children of the absent father with calls of traitor and Quisling. And what of the teacher, who instead of attempting to shield the child from abuse and even physical attack, would quietly ignore such behaviour by turning away, thereby tacitly condoning the attacks and abuse?

Fortunately, as a qualified confectioner Edith was able to find employment quite easily, but it required a thick-skin to suffer the slings of outrageous fortune that she endured during the years of my detention. She was helped by being able to return to her mother's home, where only one son remained in residence with his mother. As a farm labourer he had not been recruited into the army but did see active service in the later war years. It is a regrettable fact that the conditions of estrangement caused by detention resulted in many broken marriages, so I was more than fortunate in that mine survived.

Having stayed in Douglas during her visit in 1942, Edith returned to the same boarding house the following year. In the summer of 1945, shortly after the end of the war in Europe, I went back to the island for a nostalgic holiday, and we all stayed at the same place in Douglas. I was surprised at the friendliness of the proprietor, having expected at least some measure of coolness towards me, fortunately this was not so.

It surprises me that I have never been questioned by my many interviewers about the attitude and the feelings of the British Union detainees at the changing fortunes of the war. We had never attempted to deny our political sympathies with, and perhaps even partial support of the Lebensraum concept in German and Italian foreign policy, though we had never welcomed the prospect of an Axis military victory. If we were realists and pragmatists into the bargain, it had to be conceded that when all hope of negotiated peace had gone, an Allied victory could only result in the final defeat of our political hopes. As loyalists and patriots, an Allied defeat was totally unacceptable, but an Allied victory meant our political annihilation. I was aware of this dilemma but refused to even put the question to myself. I subconsciously dwelt on the fact that MacDonald had opposed the First World War and yet survived to become Prime Minister. I hoped that history would repeat itself.

Many years later in 1985, I made a nostalgic journey to Liverpool to seek out Danny an old Blackshirt friend. I found him, and to my surprise, after very little time he remembered me. We had not met since September 1941 when he was transferred from Peel to Brixton for his second tribunal hearing. His transfer took place only two weeks before the escape from the camp, but the interesting point is that he was the gardener in the house from which the escape was made. He did not return to Peel but was released shortly after his second hearing. It was fortunate for him that he had already left the camp, otherwise he might have been implicated in the escape, even though I knew that he did not intend to make the break. He could quite easily have been returned to Walton with me and his ultimate release might have been greatly delayed.

We had much to talk about, mostly about one-time mutual friends, many of whom are now dead. It surprised me how the mention of a name would bring a personality almost into the room with us. He even referred to the plumbing ability of my friend Ray Gauger. Danny was also an electrician, but I did not ask any questions. His wife was rather bitter about the past. Her comments bore out the points that I have already made about the trials and tribulations of the wives we left outside. My wife had two children to cater for, this lady had three.

Talking as we did about old friends reminds me how little contact I had during my detention with men like Raven Thomson, Hector McKecknie and Dick Bellamy, leading Blackshirts and old comrades. Life created its own patterns and it revolved around those with whom one was in daily contact.

One I do remember from the latter period of detention was John MacNab, at one time editor of the Fascist Quarterly, and later expelled from British Union along with Joyce. He was a very close friend of William Joyce right up to the end. I know that he regularly visited Joyce in Brixton during the time of his trial and later while awaiting execution. I still think that Joyce ought not have been hanged, victim of a dubious interpretation of the law.

Unknown to all of us at the time, William Joyce was born an

American citizen and remained so until after his flight to Germany. Once there he became a German citizen which he had every legal right to do as the United States had not then entered the war. So Joyce was hung for treason against Britain, a country of which he had never been a citizen. But his powerful enemies in this country were not going to let a little matter like that stand between William Joyce and the rope.

MacNab was a fascinating character. Highly intelligent, an Oxford-educated intellectual, but with a dour Scottish manner, yet more approachable than one would have expected. He was deeply religious and a practising Catholic. I was only a shallow practitioner in those days. My Catholicism had become over-shadowed by the more pressing demand of political expression, and MacNab was aware of this although I never thought to question how.

In conversation it emerged that Edith was non-Catholic and that we had married in the church which she attended in Churchtown, Southport. He was at great pains to remind me that in the eyes of the Catholic Church I was not married, and that on my release I ought to rectify my lapse from the true path. His arguments must have made some impression because some years later we re-married in a Catholic ceremony performed by the parish priest of Burscough Bridge where we were then in business. After the war, MacNab went to live in Spain.

The summer of 1943 passed uneventfully, one might almost say pleasantly, once one had assumed a philosophical attitude to the changing pattern in the war's progress.

It was now becoming obvious that ultimate victory would be with the allied forces, and releases were more frequent and numerous. Alamein and Stalingrad were in the main accepted as indicating the future direction that the destiny of war would take, and the political detainees could see that their release was fast becoming inevitable.

The only disturbing thought was just when it would be, and what sort of reception we could expect to meet when we returned to the outside world.

By the late summer, the numbers of British Union detainees was down to about seventy-five, and I began to consider the possibility that I might be released any day. I was afraid of sounding too optimistic about my chances when Edith made her visit, she appeared resigned to the probability that I would be among the last.

When October came and went and I was still inside, I began to think that I was destined to remain there until the end of the war, but early the next month, Oswald Mosley was released together with Lady Diana. Although this was due to health factors it seemed unlikely that any of his followers would remain imprisoned for long.

Came the day. I was arrested on June 3rd 1940, ten days after Mosley, and released in November 1943, ten days after his release from Holloway; almost three-and-a-half years of imprisonment. I was told on morning roll call to report to the main gate at midday, a sure indication of release. There was much packing to do. I entered Walton Gaol with a small attache case. I left Peel with two suitcases, and a large box. I had acquired many possessions during my imprisonment, mainly clothing and collected souvenirs from various places of detention.

I also had a business to hand over to a successor, and stocks to dispose of which had taken me months to build up. Even though I was leaving I had no wish for them to be wasted, since there were still many in the camp who could make good use of them.

Then came the emotional moment of saying goodbye to those who were left behind. When I left there were only forty-seven Mosley men left in the camp. Two other Blackshirts were being released with me, and one of them was returning to the island the following day to take up full-time employment on the farm where he had been an outside worker. There was another, and even happier reason; he intended to marry the daughter of the house, and so far as I knew this is what he did.

I reported to the gate and was given a send-off by those remaining. Personal papers including an order to report to the police of the town where I was to live, were handed to me. This instructed me to report every week under threat of re-arrest. I was handed real money, that which was standing to my credit plus the exchange of camp paper money already in my possession. It totalled £47.0.0., and made me feel quite wealthy. At least I had something tangible to show for the years that I had spent as a prisoner, but I had no idea how long it would take me to find work. There were restrictions on the type of employment open to me. In addition I was still considered a security risk, but not sufficient of course as to warrant continued detention. I then met Inspector Munt of the Metropolitan Police for the second and last time. He thanked me for not giving him cause for concern since my return to the camp, and wished me well.

We travelled in an open vehicle, in the company of two Metropolitan Police officers, to Liverpool where we were to be formally released.

The boat journey was uneventful, the most striking change being that we were free from surveillance. After three and a half years this was a strange experience.

Arriving at Liverpool Central Police Station we were met with delay, our release papers having failed to arrive from the Home Office. Peel had been instructed to release us but Liverpool had not been notified. Our hosts were in a quandary. The local police were required to issue railway travel permits but were unable to do so until we signed a paper detailing our postal address, and accepting the terms of our release.

In fact the police were in a flap since we had been released, they could no longer place us under restraint; we had been freed but they had not got the authorisation to let us go free. How typical! My first experience of democratic bureaucracy, and it was pathetic. I just laughed. The Metropolitan officers left us there and returned to Peel. So we were in a police station but not under arrest. Finally the Inspector who was brought to sort out the contretemps placed a priority call to the Home Office asking for instructions.

It was now about 5 p.m. and since most officer workers had gone home there was an inevitable delay. Eventually he was instructed to book us into an hotel, for an evening meal, bed and breakfast, and we were asked to give an undertaking to be available for collection at 9 o'clock the following morning. After the meal we went to a cinema, and the following morning given travel vouchers, and after signing a form stating the terms of our release from detention, we were freed.

I made my way to Exchange Station and substituted my travel voucher for a ticket for Southport. I was surprised that more damage had not been done to the dock area. The air raid defences had been good in view of the number of raids that Liverpool had suffered. When I arrived in Southport, where for the present I had to live, I found little change since I had left it nearly eight years before.

Chapter Four

Business Leader

IT was a little after midday and I knew that Edith would be at work and Rose at school. So after a light lunch I decided to call at Edith's place of work to let her know I was back home. The shock of seeing me without having had any prior notice was rather upsetting, and we had very little to say to one another. We had both known that the chances of my being released increased with every improvement in the war situation, but when it actually came it was still difficult to take in.

I've been very fortunate in my domestic life. I married a girl who was aware of my political activities, but who was not herself politically-minded.

My own attitude had been one of "Live for today and see what tomorrow brings". But Edith must have had one hell of a time. And yet she never uttered a single word of complaint.

The entire weight of wartime propaganda was directed against us, both as a Movement and as individuals. No matter that our opposition to the war was based on — as we saw it and still see it — a rational analysis of what that war would do to the country we loved. Among the mass of people who cared little for politics, the general thrust of Government policy and objectives was taken on trust, its correctness unquestioned. And there took root that most pernicious presumption, 'there's no smoke without fire'.

How can any man, knowing what ordeals his wife had gone through in these circumstances, convey to her, and to the public at large, the esteem in which I hold Edith? She has been the most loyal wife that any woman could ever aspire to be.

I knew it would be difficult for my mother-in-law to accept

into her house a man who had been in prison and concentration camps because of his opposition to the war, particularly as three of her sons and one of her daughters were in the armed forces.

Under the circumstances she treated me better than I expected. I was not after all, like the prodigal son who had come home repentant. It was not my home, and I was far from repentant. My children had been dumped on her, and I as their father had not contributed to their upkeep. Three and a half years of exceptional warfare conditions is a long time to avoid resentment, and when I look back I am amazed that she treated me with such consideration.

I became quite fond of the 'Old Dear', and I am glad that in some way I was able to repay some of the love and kindness that she showered upon my children during what must have been very difficult times.

It cannot have been easy for her to have to live in a small community with a son-in-law who was the talk of the village, not only while he had been away in prison, but also after his release, since it was common knowledge that I had to report to the police station every week.

She was an independent character who insisted on remaining in her little cottage in spite of her advancing years. It was a joy and delight to take her out in the car in later years. She had originated from Ironbridge and we would make an annual pilgrimage to the haunts of her youth and then take her to a hotel in Ludlow for lunch. She died when she was eighty-five; may she rest easy; she deserves to.

When I was released the war, of course, was far from over, though El Alamein and Stalingrad had pointed to its ultimate conclusion.

In those detention years my thoughts of the future were always obscure, as if I was living in a state of perpetual limbo, a return to civilian life presenting choices and decisions which I was hesitant to make. What surprised me most was that no attempt was made to enforce my registration for National Service.

Even my outspoken participation in public debate earned no official disapproval. I did observe some modicum of diplomacy always provided that this did not betray my principles and code of conduct.

It was as if I was walking a tight rope of political conscience in a hostile world, and though I made no attempt to deny my continued adherence to Mosley, I experienced very little open hostility. In the main people were prepared to concede my right to hold and express my views, provided that I refrained from expressing pro-German sympathies.

The mass of the people were very anti-German and in no way prepared to accept anything less than "Unconditional Surrender". It was to be some years before Mosley advanced his great concept of 'Europe a Nation', and until then I lived in a political vacuum. Logical thinking had compelled me to accept that a disintegrating Empire, the inevitable result of the Roosevelt-Churchill demand for unconditional surrender and the doctrine of self-determination for all, destroyed the economic basis of our pre-war policies.

The fact that Poland and all of Eastern Europe still await this right never seems to strike the people of this country as being illogical, even though the basic reason given for our declaration of war against Germany in 1939 was to free Poland from foreign occupation. It is true that Germany was destroyed, but Russia emerged as the enslaver and paramount threat to world peace, and once again we earned and deserved the title of 'Perfidious Albion'.

But returning to November 1943. I knew I would have to find

work as soon as possible. My few pounds would not last very long, and we had to decide where we were to live.

I would have been quite happy to return to Hull, though by now I had no brothers there. Peter was in the R.A.F. and his wife was working near Accrington. She and her parents had been evacuated after being bombed out of Hull. Edith did not wish to return there however, and I didn't press the point.

We gave thought to the possibility of moving to London and finally agreed I should stay for a few weeks with Sydney and look around for a suitable temporary home. I told the local police of my intention and was given permission to stay in London for two weeks after which I would have to return and report on possible moves.

I was quite excited at the prospect of living in London. If there was going to be any political activity after the war, London would be its centre and I wanted to be in the thick of it. Syd arranged for me to bunk down with him and I even worked with him for a week as a practice run.

At the first opportunity I called on an old comrade in Streatham, who had opened his small radio and record shop and was making a reasonable living. A few days before I returned I found a small furnished flat nearby and paid a week's rent in advance in the hope that Edith would agree to go.

In the event she decided not to. I had to agree it was a gamble, and it would mean she would have to give up her job. London was still being bombed, and neither of us wished to leave the children in Southport. So London was out. We decided to look for a place locally but accommodation was not easy to find.

If we were to remain in Southport however, it would be necessary to find suitable employment, and I had been out of my trade for nearly four years. Early in that New Year of 1944 we went over to Bolton to see brother Alf and his wife. Alf had remained there during the war because baking was a reserved occupation and for years he had had his own business. Since bread represented more than fifty per cent of his trade he was allowed to continue, though many private bakery businesses were closed down with the proprietors directed to work in other bakeries. It was decided that I would remain in Bolton to re-establish my confectionery expertise and that Edith and the children would come over for the weekend. This worked quite well, and I found that I had retained most of my skills, probably through my limited efforts in Peel.

At the end of the fortnight I returned to Southport. The problem now was to find congenial employment. I was determined to be a confectioner, but only bread bakers could be directed into work and all jobs were controlled by the Ministry of Labour.

So I called at the Ministry and inquired about procedures for obtaining work. The clerk behind the counter looked at me non-plussed. Such questions were not asked during the war. Individuals went where they were sent under the Direction of Labour Order-in-Council.

I repeated my question and he asked me for my National Service Number. When I told him that I hadn't one he became even more confounded, so I suggested that it might be best if I saw the manager, a proposal he didn't take kindly to. After more questions as to why I was not in the armed forces and why I had not registered for National Service, he reluctantly concluded that the situation was more than he could handle and I was directed to the office of the manager. By now I was beginning to enjoy myself. For years I had been pushed around by the Establishment and now to some degree the shoe was on the other foot.

Once in the manager's office I was offered a seat, and asked my business. I replied that I was seeking employment but of my own choosing. He looked at me rather pityingly. My choice he said was strictly limited to entry into the coal mines as an alternative to joining the army. He asked me for my National Service Number. When I replied that I hadn't one he retorted that I must, since my age group had already registered.

I countered by telling him that when my age group was due for registering, I had chosen not to do so. He looked at me more directly and asked if I was a conscientious objector, I replied that I was not. I had been willing to fight in defence of my country but I had not been prepared to register for a war fought in defence of Poland. It was like a game of 'cat and mouse', except that in this case I was the mouse and I was playing with the cat.

He then produced what he thought was his trump card. Was I aware that if I didn't accept the job to which I was directed I could be sent to prison for a month? I laughed and told him where I had been for the past three and a half years. Another month held no threat. He then altered his tactics explaining the situation that he was in, and emphasising that I must be prepared to go where I was sent. If the employer considered me unsuitable I had to report back. I agreed, fairly confident that I would be considered unsuitable after the interview with the prospective employer.

I was now prepared to try to use my detention and the pretext provided by the Home Secretary as an excuse for being declared unsuitable. I kept the appointment with the employer, a Mr. McDougal, whose business was on Lord Street and told him who I was, but made no attempt to justify my position. I even implied that I was not a bread baker but a flour confectioner and probably would not be of much use to him. To my delight, he agreed with me.

I returned to the Labour Exchange and asked the same clerk if I could see the manager. This time there was no hesitation, and I was directed to his office. When I presented the 'green card' signed by Mr. McDougal, containing my unsuitability, the manager was nonplussed. He told me that there were no other vacancies available in the baking trade in Southport but he might be successful in finding me work in Liverpool. I pointed out there were restrictions on my movements and that I had to report regularly to the police. Could I, under the circumstances, relieve him from any embarrassment by finding a job for myself? After some thought he agreed, while insisting that I report to him immediately so he could issue the necessary authorisation.

The following day I saw a vacancy notice in the window of a confectioners shop. Female confectioners could still change their employer by notification to the Labour Exchange, and so the owner had a woman in mind. But nothing ventured nothing won, so I went in and asked for the proprietor. He was a man of about my own age, exempted by his occupation from military service. He asked my business, thinking, he told me afterwards, that I was a government snooper. When I told him that I had come for the advertised job he exclaimed, "But you're a man, I can't employ you, the law doesn't allow it".

I asked him to listen to me and promised when I had finished my story I would leave if he wished. I told him I was just released from detention on the Isle of Man, that I was a qualified confectioner, a pre-war employee of Fred Halliwell, and that I would not be afraid of Mr. Halliwell's opinion as to my capabilities. I didn't suggest that Halliwell would support or even condone my political views. The owner of the shop was Vic Barker, and it was obvious that he knew Fred Halliwell, as both were members of the Southport Master Bakers' Association. My open approach seemed to have made a good impression and he told me that if I could get official approval he would give me a job. I was overjoyed and quite optimistic.

I returned after lunch and found Mr. Barker with a junior assistant. He said that he was expecting someone to call whose advice might be helpful, and that Mr. Halliwell had not hesitated to recommend me for the job.

Eventually a rather stout man came into the bakery, John Adams, secretary of the Southport Chamber of Trade, who had some influence in the commercial life of the town. He asked me a few questions about my political intentions and whether they were likely to interfere with my work. I assured him that in any event they were bound to be held in abeyance until sometime after the end of the war, and that at the moment I was only concerned in finding suitable employment. He suggested I should not return to the Labour Exchange until the following day, and in the meantime he would speak to the manager on behalf of his member, A.V. Barker.

I came to know John Adams very well indeed in the years to come, when I also became an associate member of the Southport Chamber of Trade. By a quirk of fate his son became an official of the Department of Health and Social Security, and I often met him during the years I was to sit on the appeals tribunals of the DHSS.

I went back to the Labour Exchange next morning, but this time I was a little more circumspect in my behaviour and general attitude. I had learned during the years of detention that once a point had been made it was often disadvantageous to labour it, while a little lubricant would ease an otherwise troubled situation. I had, after all, got what I set out to achieve and all that was needed was official acceptance. This came on the understanding that permission was for a limited period and could be withdrawn by the Ministry, or the employer.

So I started work the following day. I would not discuss remuneration with my employer but agreed to accept a nominal figure below the going rate for a maximum period of a month, and what he considered me to be worth at the end of that time. If I could stretch the basic allocation of raw materials with the knowledgeable infusion of unrationed substitutes which were available then I could increase profits and justify a wage well above the norm. I took on the responsibility for interviewing all representatives and the ordering of raw material. I also produced weekly production charts with detailed analysis of materials used together with stock sheets.

Within a month I had three junior assistants where he had only had one, and my employer no longer worked in the bakery. At the end of the month he paid me a wage which quite satisfied me. To be earning half a crown an hour in 1944 was well above the average even in the industrial field. After six months I was also paid a commission on increased turnover. When I left Vic Barker in 1946 I had two experienced female confectioners, and three juniors.

I often became despondent in the politically dark days of 1943-45 as the tides rolled on against almost everything I held dear by way of ambitions for my country. There were one or two bright spots however, including a meeting of ex-18b detainees in, I think, 1945. I have always revelled in emotion, and on this occasion emotion ran riot. It had been organised by George Dunlop from East London, mainly for fund-raising on behalf of Movement families in financial distress.

Some of those present were early releases, many of whom had received their call-up for National Service, while many others were in the ARP or other civilian activities. One of the diversions that evening was an impromptu concert got up by Frank Wiseman, and based on those he had arranged and compared at Ascot and Peel I was introduced as "The Demon Baker", a sobriquet I had earned at Huyton as a doughnut maker and at Peel as a maker of custard pies. I remember being repeatedly asked why I had shaved my beard!

This alas, was the last time I saw Frank Wiseman. I think he eventually got a minor teaching post in Newcastle, but nothing comparable to the post he lost upon his arrest in 1940. He was originally at Worcester Cathedral School as a music and singing tutor. Shortly before the war Frank had written, and I think composed, British Union's last marching song — "Battle Song". The words of the first verse, which even now after all these years are remembered and disturb my emotions.

"Raise aloft the standard!
The Leader marches before us!
Close up the ranks and join the chorus
Of a British battle song!
Hear the beat of the feet
Of a mighty nation waking,
Far ahead hear the tread
Of our comrades marching on.

'Gainst vested tyrants
We fight the power of gold,
With steel and sinew,
As our fathers fought of old.

The whole land re-echoes
Our grand triumphant shout;
The night of want is breaking,
Day will see their rout.

So raise aloft the standard!
The Leader marching before us!
To fight to the end
Our battalions march along."

It was with sadness that I learned about three years ago that what appeared to be all his British Union 'memorabilia' had been sold at a London auction, and I assumed he had passed on. It was rumoured that these had been bought by the Imperial War Museum. I hope so for it means that they will have been preserved for future generations to learn something from their studies of the quality of men who followed Mosley, and perhaps gain something from their example of service and sacrifice.

Detention created many individual catastrophies, and Frank Wiseman's was similar in some ways to that of Frank Hamley of Sheffield, a schoolmaster who had been arrested and searched before his class of pupils in 1940. For many years after release he was prevented from returning to his profession, in spite of his special talent in helping and educating backward and mentally handicapped children. In spite indeed! I saw Hamley on several post-war occasions. He was very active in Union Movement, and stood as Parliamentary candidate in a Northern seat in the 1960's.

By now I was keen to find a home of our own, and after some anxious moments, secured a rented cottage in Churchtown, into which we moved furniture that had been in store ever since my arrest. With life beginning to assume a regular pattern, I found that the evenings were beginning to drag.

Southport, as it happened, had one of the best debating societies in the North West, as well as a Brains Trust which met fairly regularly, and — more esoterically — a society for Psychic Research. These were to become the channels along which I pursued my need for self-expression.

I well remember the first debate I attended, the motion concerned with prisons and prison reform. After the two main speakers had presented their case, the debate was thrown open to the floor, and for the first time since my internment, I found myself rising to my feet to address a public gathering. My opening words could hardly fail to electrify the meeting! "When I was last in Walton Prison, the conditions were appalling. But if you are in prison serving a sentence because you have broken the law, then you are there legitimately and should not expect to be mollycoddled".

I cannot recall the gist of my subsequent remarks, but when the meeting was over I was asked many intimate questions, some of which I answered, others of which I avoided.

I had succeeded in doing what I wanted — to arouse interest. It is a ploy I have used over the years, and always with a measure of quiet satisfaction. I accepted an invitation to join the Debating Society, and later became its chairman for many years, until it was killed off by television in the 'sixties'.

It was about this time that I had an embarrassing experience in the town centre when I was accosted in a loud voice with the salutation "Heil Hitler". To my amazement it was Jim Battersby formerly District Leader of Southport, and pianist of exceptional ability in the different camps that we had been in.

Jim had left Peel under rather strange circumstances. I have already referred to the weirdoes of strange belief that we had in the camp, and one of them, Thomas St. Barbe-Baker, professed to believe that Adolf Hitler was the second Christ. He had a number of neophytes in the camp and sadly Jim Battersby became one of them.

He quite openly transferred his loyalty from Oswald Mosley and gave it to the German Fuhrer, and would engage unwary listeners with a diatribe on the machinations of international Jewry in its determination to prevent the second coming of the Messiah. After Stalingrad and Alamein Jim became very depressed and was transferred to the care of the medics. He was later moved back to the mainland and after medical treatment, released. I later heard that he had been separated from his wife but was not aware that he was living in Southport. I originally had a high regard not only for his musical skills but also for his intelligence. I could never understand how he ever came under the spell of the crackpot Hitler worshipper.

When I saw Jim in town on subsequent occasions I would do my best to avoid him and his absurd and embarrassing salutations. Regrettably he came to an untimely end, taking his own life by jumping overboard from the Mersey Ferry Boat into the revolving paddles at the rear. The stress and strain of detention and marital problems, coupled with unrealistic and mentally unbalanced political views, eventually became more than he could bear.

I sometimes felt guilty in that I had not tried to influence his thinking into more rational channels. I was more concerned in making my own life more bearable in frustrating times. The Allied landings in Normandy were now beginning to show slow but realistic progress, and it was becoming even more clear that it would only be a question of time before the ultimate German collapse.

I would still catch the voice of William Joyce broadcasting from Deutschlandsender, and on April 30 1945 heard a voice which I later learned was that of Admiral Doenitz say, "der Fuhrer ist tot, der Fuhrer ist tot". I called through to the kitchen where Edith was preparing a meal, and told her that it had just been announced on German radio that Hitler was dead. To my surprise I never met any of the original Southport British Union members, except Mr. Harris who I had met last seen at Ascot Camp. On the rare occasions I saw him now he was not inclined to talk, which was perhaps understandable. He lived with his elderly mother who had suffered mentally as a result of his imprisonment.

However, I did meet two friends from my detention days, both of whom were Anglo-Germans. My wife and I had been to a show at the Garrick Theatre, and as we were leaving I was tapped on the shoulder and a soft voice said "Wie geht es, lieber freundin?", and on turning round I saw Rudolf Deitz from Liverpool, and Freddie Gebhardt from Leeds. Gebhardt was staying in Liverpool with his friend and had come over to Southport just for the evening. It was quite a coincidence that we should meet so unexpectedly. We could not talk for long as they were hurrying to the station to get the train for Liverpool. I did not see them again.

I enjoyed my sessions with the society and meeting some of the well-known personalities whom I debated against. One of the most enjoyable from a personal satisfaction angle was my debate with Hannen Swaffer.

I do not remember the actual subject but it was concerned with nationalisation of the major industries, and my argument was that nationalisation stifled personal initiative and in so doing destroyed ambition, depriving that nation of its driving force.

I won the debate with an overwhelming vote. My debate with Leary Constantine, the West Indian cricketer, and later politician, was concerned with the British Government's failures to sustain and improve social conditions in the colonies and the need to prevent racial discrimination. He had expressed the wish that there be no vote at the conclusion of the debate. I remember him as a most sincere speaker and a very likeable person.

I lost my debate against Jenny Lee, wife of Nye Bevan. She had a very penetrating style of delivery and in her discourse made a somewhat derogatory remark about Oswald Mosley which rather annoyed me as I felt that the comment was out of context. She referred to his sojourn in both the Conservatives and the Labour parties, and the failure of his New Party. I suspect that she had been primed before the debate that I was a Mosley supporter though she made no actual reference to it.

What a contrast between her and Bessie Braddock! Bessie was just a crude, illiterate braggart. How she ever came to marry Jack Braddock, who was light years ahead of her intellectually, was something I never understood. He was a first-class debater. I lost to him as well, but this did not give me cause for concern. I was of those strange political animals whose basic philosophy was socialist, but one to whom nationalisation was anathema. I always admired Jack Braddock. He should have been the member for Kirkdale, not Bessie.

I remember an occasion during a post-war general election when Jack Bonney stood as Labour candidate for Southport, and Bessie Braddock attended the eve of poll meeting at the Cambridge Hall. There was a rather persistent interrupter in the audience who annoyed Bessie during her address. She came to the front of the platform and bawled out in a loud voice, "Thee shurrup", which I am sure cost Jack Bonney a lot of votes.

I had known Jack Bonney for a number of years. He had for many years been chairman of the debating society, and was an up-and-coming solicitor working in the offices in Liverpool of Sydney Silverman and operating in tandem with Rose Heilbron against whom I also on one occasion debated. She won too. Miss Heilbron was later to become Britain's first woman King's Counsel. She had a brilliant analytical brain, and was a fascinating speaker. Silverman of course was the MP for Colne Valley for many years. I met him once and was not particularly impressed. Jack Bonney had been a member of the short-lived Common Wealth Party. He tried to interest me in its programme in view of the apparent death knell of Mosley's hopes and I briefly studied its policy. It had been launched by Sir Richard Acland as a sort of nostalgic alternative to the disintegration of the Empire but he soon abandoned it after realising its impracticality.

Now at last came the end of the war, and with it a great outpouring of popular jubilation. The Chief Constable wrote to inform me that with the ending of the "State of Emergency" I was no longer required to report to the police.

Free for the first time since June 1940, I was almost in a celebratory mood, but though as a patriot I shared much of the general feeling, also as a patriot and I believe, a realist, I knew that it was largely a pyrrhic victory.

We had certainly brought about the defeat of Nazi Germany, but in so doing had reduced Britain to a near-bankrupted nation dependent on American aid, no longer able to hold the Empire together, and for ever after a third rank country.

What a paradox that a war which saw our "greatest hour" should prove to be our greatest undoing, and that a Prime Minister who stomped around growling about his resolute attachment to the greatness of Britain and the continuity of her Empire, should have been the chief instrument in the destruction of both!

And while this was taking place, the nations of Eastern Europe who the British politicians and Establishment had claimed to have fought a war to protect, were going over one by one to the slave masters of the Soviet Union.

All this had been foreseen by Oswald Mosley and British Union; loss of Empire, loss of British independence, and the rise to world dominance of the United States and the Soviet Union. One day an impartial historical judgement will re-assess the respective strategic policies of Churchill and Mosley, but at present, some 45 years after the end of that foolish, avoidable and disastrous war, the subject is still cocooned in a carefully-preserved mythology, and protected — as the case of the British publishing and press boycott of David living's "Churchill's War" confirms, by an Establishment, all-party censorship.

Many of these thoughts occupied my mind as I watched the bunting go up over the streets. There was always the feeling that the war could have been avoided with dignity and honour, and millions of lives spared. It is almost impossible to describe this feeling to anyone who has not been in similar circumstances. It was as if conscience was at war with itself.

I had not wanted a German victory, and yet I could not experience any sense -of satisfaction or joy at its defeat. It was a most unpleasant experience. I knew that I had to accommodate my thinking and indeed my whole life, to an unwanted situation, and I did not know how I was going to cope. I feel I was in some way a hypocrite, and to me hypocrisy is the vilest of all human wickedness.

By October 1945 the debating season was once again in full swing. I was invited to participate in a Brains Trust session one night, the subject of which was the Nuremberg Trials and related issues. These events were usually reported in the local press, and I hit the headlines as "John Charnley, member of the local Brains Trust claims to have known William Joyce". This came about because I had attacked the principle of retrospective trials. Quite unblushingly, I gave it as my opinion that when Joyce entered Germany late in 1939, he did so from a genuine desire to halt the slide into war, and that for this he should not be condemned.

Shortly after I was asked if I would be willing to debate the Jewish question. I agreed to do so and thereafter much time was spent on the wording of the motion, which finally emerged as "That anti-Semitism can be justified".

Southport has always had a fairly large Jewish community, and the press adverts for the debate caused quite a furore. Attempts were made to get the debate stopped. Then the proprietors of the restaurant where it was scheduled to take place were asked to cancel the engagement, but this would have been in breach of a long-term contract. Then approaches were made to compel the police to get the debate banned, but under existing legislation they had no power to do so.

A few days before the debate the police arrived at my work, to tell me they would be in attendance and that I should be wary in my handling of the proceedings. Came the night of the debate, and the room was packed, with people standing at the rear. At the front were many Jews, who had been queuing well in advance of the meeting.

My opponent was a well-known local Jew whose name escapes me. He had a reputation as a good speaker. Opening the debate, I was aware I would need to temper my usual aggressive style if I was to succeed in getting a hearing. Sensing a subdued apprehension as I rose, I began by seeking to gain the audience's sympathy stressing the need for an understanding of the cause of anti-Jewish feeling in numerous countries and over many centuries. I suggested that the constant repetition of persecutions such as that carried out in the reign of Henry VII must in itself denote some Jewish blame. To my pleasant surprise I was given a fair hearing, but there was little applause as I resumed my seat.

My opponent was more vitriolic in style, thereby giving me some grudging sympathy. He did, however, turn some of my arguments against me by suggesting that subconscious behaviour on the one part would not spark off violent opposition on the other, unless there was an inhibited desire for such a reaction. When the debate was thrown open I was surprised by the measure of support I received, giving me in the end, one third of the votes. The debate was well reported not only in the Southport press but in the Liverpool newspapers as well.

Anti-Semitism of course, is a subject that figures prominently in any analysis of the Mosley Movement. In my numerous conversations with O.M. the Jewish question was never once discussed. As a matter of strict record, it was not until the Albert Hall speech of April 1934 — some 18 months after the founding of British Union — that Mosley first mentioned the Jews in a public speech, and this was to note that Jews were heavily conspicuous among those convicted by the courts for violence against individual Blackshirts, and disruptive and violent behaviour at Blackshirt meetings. Mosley also drew the attention of his audience to the growing Jewish campaign against Germany, and the danger this held for dragging Britain into a war. "We fought Germany once before in a British quarrel, we shall not fight her a second time in a Jewish quarrel", he told the thousand who packed the Hall that night. Fair enough.

It cannot be denied however that numbers of Mosley's supporters were anti-Jewish, some more blatantly than others. It was my own experience that openly-expressed anti-Semitism was far more evident in those areas where Jews constituted a large gathering in a restricted area.

Mosley's condemnation of Jewish anti-Blackshirt violence and his attack on Jewish financial interests in the City of London unquestionably led to open expression of anti-Jewish hostility from many speakers. I must include myself in their number, though I always endeavoured to preface my remarks with a condemnation of specific behaviour by a section of the Jewish community.

When I paid my first visit to the Blackshirt headquarters in Southport in 1933, I sought and was given assurances that the Mosley Movement was not anti-Semitic. Yet there is no disputing that in the hectic years that followed, my own attitude underwent a change. No doubt personal experience had much to do with it, as well as my endorsement of Mosley's denunciation of finance and the Jewish mobilisation of anti-German policies and attitudes.

I was beaten up by a Jewish mob in Bury New Road and thrown through a shop window. Nine months later I moved to Hull, where intense political activity brought me into contact with members of the local Communist Party, many of whom were Jews. It is interesting to note in passing, that in his recent autobiography, the journalist and newspaper personality Derek Jameson said that nearly all the Communists in East London in the early post-war years were Jewish. I was involved in a number of scuffles with Jewish Communists over the years, and all encouraged the development of anti-Jewish sentiments which found expression at the many meetings I addressed. I heard Mosley address many hundreds of meetings however, and not once did I hear him utter any statement that could be described as anti-Semitic, although on numerous occasions he attacked with the full force of his rhetorical powers, Jewish money power.

My life was quite pleasant and work enjoyable when out of the blue, nemesis struck. While busy in the bakery one morning, a man carrying a small brief case appeared at the door and told me he was the new manager. I was dumbstruck, and when at last it penetrated my bemused brain that he was not joking, I reacted rather cruelly.

I knew my staff, and knew I had their loyalty. I told the girls to stop work, turned to the intruder and said, "Right. Start managing", and sat down. Deflated, he appealed to me to accept the situation. Assuming that I had been forewarned of the change, he had not anticipated my reactions, and agreed to fetch Vic Barker to explain to me in person what was going on.

He came within the hour, by which time we had resumed normal production. Barker reassured me that my salary would remain unchanged, and that I would continue as foreman in charge of the girls. But I remained perplexed over the motives behind the action, and knew that we had reached a parting of the ways. And so during the lunch break I slipped to the estate agent next door to ask whether he had any suitable business for sale. I had decided that if I could make profits for an employer there was no reason why I couldn't make them for myself.

A few weeks later I received details of a mixed grocery and bakery business in the nearby village of Burscough Bridge. I contacted Vincent, who for years had been a grocery manager for one of the multiples, and he responded enthusiastically to the idea of a partnership, he to run the shop and Edith and I the bakery. Unfortunately, I possessed just £75 to set against the purchase price of £7,500, a very great deal of money in 1946.

Not a promising position from which to embark on a business venture!

I pressed on however. Vincent agreed to put up half the deposit, leaving me to find the balance. Before committing myself I went to see Fred Halliwell, my employer of the mid-thirties, who listened sympathetically. He told me to go ahead, and impressed on me that if I was to succeed there was one thing I must always remember; sentiment has no place in business.

Equipped with a philosophy which in most respects ran counter to my own, I still had my share of the deposit to find. My old landlady had been so kind in my earlier days in Southport, and it was to her that I went. "How much do you want?" was her immediate response. I told her, and she asked me to return the following day when I could have it. Two days later I paid the deposit, and shortly after secured a mortgage. The next Monday I handed in my notice. I was never to work for another man again.

Even my introduction to business life had to commence in a difficult fashion. My brother and I were due to take over the business at the end of September, and our arrangements had originally been geared to this date. Rationing was still in force, and the country was beginning to feel the effect of being a post-war pauper nation. Pre-war foreign investments had all been liquidated to pay for the war, and we were dependent on America for extended credits to maintain the food rations.

Early in July 1946, the Government had been forced to introduce bread rationing, something which had been avoided throughout the entire war period. It was quite unexpected, and the announcement that bread rationing would start on July 16th precipitated the retirement of Mr. Wells, from whom we were buying the business, and we had to assume control of the business at a few day's notice.

Our finances were already stretched to the limit, and we opened the shop with a float of exactly ten pounds, which we raised by the sale of a spare tyre to the local garage proprietor.

We literally had no reserves and were entirely dependent on day-to-day sales in the shop and from the two vans to keep the business going. Government restrictions were making their influence felt in other areas of our new business. Only two sizes of bread loaf were permitted, their prices fixed at below-production cost, and the balance made up by a subsidy. This created a cash flow problem, and overall those early post-war years were very difficult for the small trader.

In the past I had been something of a 'Don Quixote', and it was going to be hard to accept this new principle of 'dog eat dog' as a permanent pattern of life. My father had told me when I was very young that the truly honest man seldom succeeded in business, and Fred Halliwell had assured me in his advice only a few months ago that sentiment had no place.

I was already beginning to doubt if I was really cut out for the business life. Money had few attractions for me. I had never wanted to be rich, and I could not see myself as a burgeoning entrepreneur, but I did relish the thought of financial independence and wanted to escape permanently from the danger of the cavalier treatment of the Vic Barkers of this world.

It soon became evident that business would serve a purpose if it enabled me to enter wide spheres of activity, when such talents as I possessed might be put to a more unselfish purpose.

I did not know that the future was to provide the vehicle which I was to ride for over thirty years. I am fortunate that the very living of those years and the service which I gave were in themselves very gratifying, though any recognition I received was mainly conspicuous by its absence, with one special exception.

One evening Vincent handed me a leaflet announcing a public meeting in Ormskirk to which all traders and business people were invited. Its purpose was to launch a local Chamber of Trade, an area of life about which I knew little. I did however recollect my meeting with John Adams, secretary of the Southport Chamber of Trade, so out of curiosity Vincent and I went along to the meeting. It was a move that was to set me on a 30 year programme of interesting, and I hope, useful activity.

The well-attended meeting in Church House was organised under the banner of the Council of Retail Distributors, a body backed by the Daily Express, with Lord Beaverbrook financing two or three national organisers. One of them was Lionel Fowler, who I was to come to know quite well. I was elected to the steering committee, and in February 1947 the South West Lancashire Chamber of Commerce was officially launched with Glyn Hughes, a local chemist, as our first president, and J. Irving Lace, an accountant, as first secretary. Affiliation to the Council of Retail Distributors (C.O.R.D.), entitled us to attend area council meetings and I was appointed the official delegate to represent the Chamber.

This was the time of the first majority Labour Government, and we were being swamped with socialist legislation on an unprecedented scale, even though Labour's parliamentary vote had only been 49%. Our voting system is such that a minority vote on a national scale can result in an overwhelming allocation of Party seats in Parliament. I was watching the political scene with growing interest, and awaiting news of Mosley's re-entry into the arena, although I realised that now I was in business I might have to be circumspect in the expression of my views.

Mosley had already produced his first post-war book, 'My Answer', which rebutted his critics on the question of his pre-war stand, and prepared the way for another which was to appear the following year entitled 'The Alternative'.

With my new involvement in business affairs I at last found what I had been deprived of since June 1940: a platform whereon I could declaim, and explain, and fulminate, on a variety of economic subjects dear to my heart.

I was a retail trader, an accomplished baker, a practical grocer, and into the bargain an adept debater to whom the platform became almost my reason for living. I realised then that to me, business was only the means whereby I could continue to use my talents to further my own well-being, and satisfy my ego.

Shortly after the formation of the South West Lancashire Chamber I met Harold Wilson. He was the first of many leading politicians I was to meet over the next thirty years. Wilson had been elected as Member of Parliament for the Ormskirk Division in the 1945 election and the Prime Minister Clement Attlee had appointed him President of the Board of Trade.

Food rationing was still very much in force, and a butcher was only allowed to operate a butchery business provided that he had a licence issued by the Ministry. If a Master Butcher were to fall foul of the numerous inspectors who harassed every shopkeeper who doled out the meagre rations of the day, he could have his licence taken away and lose his business.

A local butcher who was a member of his National Federation and also a member of the local Chamber of Trade, had offended against the stringent rationing laws. Threatened with loss of his licence and business, he had been given three weeks to lodge an appeal. Mr. Scott brought the matter before the next meeting of the executive committee and it was agreed we send a deputation to London to see Harold Wilson on our member's behalf. There were four of us, D.C.M. Scott, Glynn Hughes, Eric Waiting and myself — butcher, chemist, gent's outfitter and grocer-baker. We met Mr. Wilson in the Board of Trade offices up Horse Guards Parade, and he did not impress me at all. If he was typical of the calibre of Ministerial rank in the Government of the day, then I had grave fears for our future national economy and rewards for personal initiative. He was a perfect example of the cliché-spouting demagogue spawned by doctrinaire socialism, and I took an instant dislike to him. I have not revised my first assessment. His ultimate action in his abrupt departure from the occupancy of 10, Downing Street struck me as being quite in keeping with his behaviour on the occasion of our meeting in 1947.

We were unsuccessful in our attempts to save the licence of our member and his business continued under another name, although he was appointed its manager. When rationing was finally abandoned, he reacquired control of the business, without any overt departure from legalistic requirements.

The chamber was recognised as a body of representative business interests in the town and as such asked to accept membership of various quasi government bodies. Again it fell to me to fill these appointments because I seemed able to fit them into my working schedule. My first was to the local Committee for Employment of Disabled Persons, with regular meetings held in Southport, followed by a term with the Gas Consultative Council with meetings in Liverpool.

Membership of the former required visiting disabled persons in their home, and in many instances I was reminded of my earlier commitment to visits of this nature during my pre-war association with the Society of St. Vincent de Paul in Southampton. In some instances the disabled were casualties of the war, but often the disability would be of a genetic nature and the multiple sclerosis cases could be quite harrowing.

It was important to adopt an attitude not in any way patronising and yet to show genuine concern. There were so many instances where employment of even a most casual kind could become an unhoped for boon in a life which otherwise held no meaning or purpose.

I suppose in one sense, particularly in my early political activities, I have been somewhat brash and deliberately provocative. But uncaring I have never been, and I found it increasingly hard to remain objective and unemotional. I was relieved when my term of service on this committee ended and I somewhat guiltily informed the chairman that I would not be available for reappointment.

I served two terms on the Gas Consultative Council, but eventually withdrew since its title was a misnomer. The committee were never really consulted. We would be informed of the future plans of the Regional Gas Board and invited to discuss them with officials, but decisions had been taken before the proposals reached the discussion stage. I eventually realised that the Council was only a facade or sop to sweeten the public in favour of acceptance of programmes which otherwise would have generated opposition.

During this time I was still attending the Friday evening meetings of the debating Society of which I was now a speaker of some repute. These were a welcome relief from the hectic business life I was leading. There were two debates from the period which remain quite vividly in my memory. One was on the inevitability of war, when one of the principal speakers was the late Fenner Brockway, of the Independent Labour Party. He had at one time been a close associate of Oswald Mosley in his Labour Party days. Brockway was quite an impressive speaker with an unusual style and very persuasive and logical in the presentation of his argument. I would have welcomed an opportunity for a more intimate talk but unfortunately he had to return to London the same night. I was surprised when he finally accepted a peerage on his retirement from the House of Commons, but by so doing he did at least retain some semblance of involvement with the political scene.

The other debate which stands out in my memory was on euthanasia. We had experienced no difficulty in finding a speaker in favour of the subject, but we were concerned as to the debating ability of an opposing speaker.

The chairman, Jack Bonney, suggested we approach a Catholic priest who might be willing to accept the challenge. I was not at this time practising my faith but was in agreement with the suggestion, and agreed to try to find a priest able and willing to fit the bill.

For a Catholic priest to speak from a public platform in those days required sanction from his immediate senior, and I had been given the name of a priest who was reputedly a good speaker. He was only a curate, however, and his parish priest was not noted for his magnanimity. However, I decided to see him. He was a Father Collins, curate at St. Joseph's Birkdale, Southport. A few weeks previously he had been a member of the local Brains Trust at which I had also spoken, so I was convinced that, provided he was willing to accept the invitation, we would be assured of a good night.

I called at the Presbytery one afternoon and asked for Father Collins. He came to the door and immediately I experienced an unusual rapport. I seemed to be in contact with a kindred spirit. He asked me my business and I told him it was of an unusual nature, not directly connected with religious matters, but one in which I was convinced he would hold strong views. I told him I was there on behalf of the Southport Debating Society, and we wanted him to speak in a debate. When I told him I had been on the local Brains Trust and that my name was Charnley, he looked at me more closely and said, "Are you the man who claimed to have known William Joyce?" This broke the ice, and after some further questioning as to timing and general procedure, he agreed, subject to the approval of his parish priest. He rang a few days later, accepting. The debate was held a few weeks later and he put up a splendid performance, carrying his point with a reasonable majority when it came to the vote. I was not expecting to see him again except perhaps at a future debating session, but I did, and under circumstances of near tragedy.

I was becoming too optimistic, and in October 1947, fate was ready to strike again. Edith and I, together with Vincent, had gone to see a play at The Little Theatre in Southport and during the interval I was taken ill. When we got home my doctor came to see me. He diagnosed appendicitis and a serious hernia condition, and this meant hospital and surgery. He recommended a Liverpool surgeon, Philip Hoare, and fortunately for me he was a good one. I was now going to have to pay the price of all those years of detention when I was denied adequate medical treatment for a gradual worsening bowel condition which had probably exacerbated the hernia weakness. At least, that's what the surgeon told me many months afterwards when I went for a check-up. He greeted me with the words, "Ah, here comes the man who should not be alive".

However, returning to the sequence of events, I was admitted to hospital almost immediately and operated on the following day. Everything seemed satisfactory until some five days later when I began to experience intense discomfort in a greatly distended stomach. In addition I was being sick and turning yellow.

I realised that Edith was very concerned, and after undergoing some X-rays, an urgent call was put through to Mr. Hoare the surgeon. There was now some urgency in my situation, it was decided that if Mr. Hoare was unavailable, the local surgeon, Mr. Hunter, would operate.

In the meantime my doctor, J.J. Rogan, knowing that I was a Catholic, albeit a non-practising one, sent for a priest, but without informing me. This was Father Formby, a parish priest of St. John's Burscough Bridge, whom I had met on a few occasions. His arrival non-plussed me and I refused to talk. It was a reaction he had not expected, but in spite of this, Fr. Formby urged me to think of my religious faith of the past, and to accept his ministrations.

In the matter of the Last Rites, the Catholic reader will understand the problem faced by a priest in trying to overcome the inbuilt pride and arrogance of the recalcitrant recusant. I realise now that I was, to say the least, very rude and obdurate. However, by dint of faith and understanding, he broke down my resistance to the extent that I said I would see one priest if he could be persuaded to come; Father Collins. He promised he would try to make contact, but I did not expect to see the parish priest from St. Joseph's Birkdale. Dr. Rogan now came in to tell me my condition was critical and I would be returning to the theatre for further surgery. Mr. Hoare was located at a Liverpool social function and arrived in my ward in white tie and tails.

Meanwhile my priest friend from Southport had arrived, cycling from Birkdale in pouring rain to answer a call from a person he had met only once. He told me many months later that he could not even remember me until he saw me, and reminded him of the debate on euthanasia. To receive the Last Rites of the Church is a peculiarly moving experience. I have been the recipient on four occasions, so I suppose I've had some close shaves over the past forty years.

When Father Collins left me, Mr. Hoare arrived at my bedside to tell me that for some reason, which he did not at the moment understand, I appeared to have developed a complete blockage of the bowels which required immediate surgery. My condition was very grave and he was anxious that I fully appreciate the seriousness of the situation.

He emphasised that he was going to be very frank. He was a great believer in the power of the mind as an aid to surgery, and if I wanted to live I would have to fight. He understood that in the past I had been a noted fighter but that this would be my greatest battle. He also understood that I was a Catholic and that the priest had just left me.

Did I know that the Matron of the hospital and the night sister were also Catholics, as was my own doctor? He was telling me this because they were all going to assist in the operation. He wanted me to know that I only had one chance in a hundred of surviving the operation. I had to understand that I was a member of that team, albeit a passive one, but I could make a valid contribution if I willed myself to survive. If I could overcome the operation, and the nursing staff could maintain my life until morning, my chances of survival would be fifty-fifty, and each day the odds would improve.

I previously had little experience of the medical profession, and to be addressed in this manner was so dramatic and shattering that I had very little to say except that I appreciated the frankness of what he was saying. "Yes! I did want to live, there was so much that I wanted to do".

For six weeks after that operation I had nothing to eat or drink, but was fed by saline drip into the vein and a constant supply of blood intravenously fed. Every few hours I was pumped clear of stomach fluids through a 'Riles Tube', this being the most unpleasant aspect of the long, slow period of recovery.

I went into hospital weighing 9st. 8lbs, and came out weighing 5st. 3lbs, after a stay of nine weeks. Every evening Edith came to see me, and I used to plead with her to swab out my mouth with damp cotton wool because it tasted so foul, and she would do as I begged, though awfully afraid in case I swallowed any water in the process. The bowel had to remain completely immobile to enable scar tissue to heal, and it was a long slow process.

Many nights I lay in that bed feeling that I would not see the dawn. I was told afterwards that brother Peter remained in the waiting room throughout the whole of the first night, while Edith waited by the telephone at home hoping that it would not ring. I was also told later that when I was returned to the ward the Matron and the night Sister sat at my bedside each holding one of my hands and clasping their own hands across my bed.

Is there any truth in the theory of the life cycle flowing between the living and the almost dead? If there is, then I must be an example of it, because I had an unusual experience of hovering over my own body and seeing myself lying there and wondering if I would ever re-occupy that body. It was perhaps a dream, but was it?

Convalescence was a long, slow process, and the fight back to full health a difficult one, though I did attempt to pick up my Chamber of Trade activities at both local and area level. In April 1948 Edith and I went down to Cornwall, to stay with Charlie Watts, a Blackshirt friend who had a small guest house in Mousehole, just outside Penzance, where we stayed for three weeks. In spite of the food rationing Charlie managed to keep a good table and I slowly began to regain some of the weight I had lost during my long stay in hospital.

Charlie, who had been District Leader of British Union's Westminster St. George branch and organiser of the successful London Cabmen's Group, was a great character, well-known and popular in London in pre-war days. In 1940, he was one of a selected few of British Union who were taken to the notorious Latchmere House, Ham Common, the home of that Government department where weeks of psychological torture, in a semi-starvation regime of solitary confinement, was practised to force 'confessions', as they did there with a number of German spies. They did not 'break' Charlie. He, in fact, broke his interrogators, but in the process over the three week 'course' his dark hair turned to greying-white.

Shortly after returning home from Cornwall I was appointed local Chamber delegate to the annual C.O.R.D. conference at Brighton. I have been to many conferences over the past 35 years, but none was so enjoyable as this.

I confess that I remember little of the business conducted during the daily sessions. I was still a comparative newcomer to trade politics but I was an avid pupil and appreciated only too well that here was the type of platform which I would eventually make my own

In the not too distant future were the days when I would be cheered as I made my way to the microphone, in anticipation of my contribution to the subject matter under debate, particularly if it was known that I was to be provocative in my deliver. But this was my first conference and I was still finding my feet. The street corner harangue could, if used with circumspection, still make its initial impact, but a lasting impression could only be created if oratory was combined with logic and knowledge of one's subject. My debating skills acquired and developed over the years were now beginning to find their true outlet, because I could combine a fluent tongue with sincere belief.

It was here that I first met Ernest Marples, the Wallasey MP who was the guest speaker. He was a handsome man, with a commanding appearance who spoke with consummate skill. This was in the heyday of Clem Attlee's post-war socialist government, so there was naturally much that the dominant and thrusting Conservative Parliamentarian could offer to an audience generally anti-socialist.

It was an opportunity that Marples did not miss. He gave a first-class address, well calculated to ensure growing support for H.M. opposition, and naturally supporting the basic economic ideas that would please an audience whose livelihood depended on private enterprise.

I met him on a number of occasions in later years when he became a Minister in the Conservative Government. I was surprised at his early retirement from the political field. I had known, of course, of his French vineyards, but assumed that it was only a hobby, and did not anticipate that he would decide to retire permanently to France. He was the first Member of Parliament to entertain me to afternoon tea on the Terrace of the House. The occasion brought back my youthful dreams. This was where I, too, had thought to disport myself!

It should not be thought that I had forgotten or deserted my political loyalties in favour of easier roads to travel. Far from it. For some time I had been in receipt of the monthly Mosley News Letter, published in 1946-1948, giving Oswald Mosley's interpretation of post-war political events and his endeavours to answer some of the newly emerging problems.

Then, in November of 1947, he published The Alternative which I read with an almost greedy anticipation. With the Empire virtually abandoned or liquidated, it was clear that the pre-war policy of a viable economy operating within an insulated Empire was no longer possible. And so I read with interest and a growing conviction, that concept of 'Europe a Nation'; a strategy for the post-war world that was not only feasible but also more desirable than the improvised status quo of a beleaguered island off the continental land mass, dependent on 'hand-outs' from our wealthy relative across the Atlantic.

I think it was in 1946 that I met O.M. for the first time since that very emotional encounter before the great East London Peace Demonstration in May 1940, just weeks before the mass arrest of leading British Union members.

The venue was Mosley's flat in Dolphin Square, London, and was the first time that I met Lady Mosley. Dolphin Square, as it happened, was the scene of Mosley's arrest, and three and a half years later, during my internment, I missed him by a few weeks following his transfer to Holloway.

His obvious pleasure at seeing me again, and the smile of welcome on his face was almost more than I could bear. He introduced me to his wife, saying, "This is Charnley, of whom I have spoken to you, one of my most loyal supporters in the North. This is his wife. They have two young children". Edith often recalls that occasion and the deep impression Lady Mosley made on her. Of the meeting itself I remember little. There were not many of us there, perhaps a dozen including Captain Hamer, George Dunlop, who administered the distribution of help to needy families of British Union detainees, Mick Clarke and Charlie Hammond.

All that I can recall of his general remarks was that the pre-war policies of the Movement were no longer applicable to post-war economic conditions, and he was finalising his thinking on a new approach to the changed situation and urgent problems of the immediate post-war world.

It was a time of nostalgia, just as it is now as I write. I recall a sentence or two from his autobiography "My Life" in which he said, "I was always pleased beyond any other praise when a working man would come up to me after a meeting and say, 'You have been saying what I have felt all my life.' My speech must have touched some deep chord within the eternal spirit of England. This is not sentiment, this is reality. This is the force which moves men."

My senses have always been susceptible to the human voice, especially the singing voice, but that which penetrated my heart and reached every fibre of my being was that of Oswald Mosley; when he hurled his challenge unto the winds of destiny at the Royal Albert Hall in April 1934, on the numerous great meetings and demonstrations in East London, and in that vast hall at Earls Court only a few weeks before Churchill's Bloody War. Oh, that the people of Britain had heeded that voice! How different would our lives be today.

The publication of "The Alternative" was followed shortly after by a meeting at which the press were present, and which I also attended. The venue was Mosley's home then in London, and Picture Post, popular illustrated magazine, published by Hulton Press, went to town on the issue, devoting much of the central space to photographs of Mosley's Lieutenants', including comments from each.

I was included in the list, and this was to create something of a furore in our Chamber of Trade. Some of the executive members seemed to believe they were being infiltrated by fascist subversives, and as a result I was asked to attend a special meeting of the committee to give an account of my actions.

I was a little surprised at the amount of resentment levelled against me in the initial lead-up to the meeting, because I had not anticipated that feelings could be so intense. For the first time I was made to realise and appreciate how successful the channels of wartime propaganda had been, and still were, in sowing the seeds of hatred.

The meeting was opened by Glyn Hughes, the President, who after showing me a copy of Picture Post carrying my photograph and comments, asked me to give an explanation. I was, he said, already known as the accredited delegate to area and national meetings, and it was necessary to ensure that the local Chamber was not in any way being used as a neo-fascist platform.

I told my fellow committee members that I, like them, had helped to form the Chamber because I believed that in so doing I was contributing to the strengthening of private enterprise and personal initiative, and that they had appointed me to the position of delegate because they believed that such talents as I had might be exploited in that direction.

I went on to say that while I had never denied my association with Oswald Mosley, I had never made use of any opportunity to express my political views on any Chamber of Trade platform.

I stressed that although I had spent nearly four years in various prisons and camps, no attempt had ever been made to prefer charges against me, nor had my loyalty to my country ever been questioned. I went on to quote Walpole, Chatham, Charles James Fox, Lloyd George and Ramsay McDonald, all of whom had opposed wars in which England had been engaged, and to declare that I was doing no more than historical precedent justified. I gave an undertaking that at no time in the future would I use a Chamber of Trade occasion to express my politics, but that I was not prepared to turn my back on Oswald Mosley or repudiate my loyalty to him.

As soon as I had finished, D.C.M. Scott rose to his feet and to my surprise thanked me for my honesty. Loyalty, he said was a trait of character he had always admired, and felt certain that the same loyalty would always be used in support of the local Chamber and he would propose a vote of full confidence in their debate. The President took the unusual step of seconding the motion and when put to a vote it was carried unanimously. Thereafter I successfully blended my trade and my political activities throughout thirty-five years, without any further open hostility or even argument or discussion.

In the days immediately after the war, Britain's politicians proceeded as if nothing had changed in our national circumstances and our relationship with the rest of the world. Some indeed rather assumed that we had acquired a unique role in global affairs. Many people went along in this belief. After all, had we not just won a war?

I do not think it is excessive to claim that Mosley was alone in perceiving the underlying reality. The post-war world indeed, had moved into precisely the pattern he had forecast in 1939-40 when he warned that Britain's entry into a foreign quarrel would lead to its rapid decline, economically and politically.

Such was our fate in 1945-46, a position that the subsequent years were to confirm. While our country was reduced to penury and utter dependence on American aid, the foundations of our once great Empire weakened beyond recall, with one third of

Continental Europe under Russian control or quaking before the prospect, two great powers had pushed Britain aside and were now dictating terms to the rest of the world; the United States and Soviet Russia. Such was Churchill's legacy!

So far as the Mosley Movement was concerned, it was clear that many of the fundamentals of our pre-war policies were no longer viable, above all the concept of Britain at the centre of a self-contained, economically insulated Empire. The British Empire was not the least of the victims of the Second World War, and economic nationalism was dead.

How soon Mosley realised this I do not know, but it was not many months after the war's conclusion that he began to write and speak about an extension of patriotism, and a move beyond Fascism and Democracy into a new philosophy that addressed the grave condition and issues before us.

In late 1947 this led to Mosley's great vision of Europe a Nation, a concept which lay at the heart of the new post-war Union Movement, which Mosley launched in February 1948.

As a successor to our pre-war position, it seemed to me to be perfectly logical, though others, many of them fine pre-war stalwarts, were to find the switch from British Empire to United Europe impossible to accept. Though their emotional loyalty to Oswald Mosley remained, their political commitment faded. They simply could not bring themselves to accept that the world had changed, and with it the challenge to new ideas. Mosley referred to his new post-war European philosophy as an extension of Patriotism. I called it natural progression of history using the example of the development of the Saxon Heptarchy in the creation of a United Kingdom under Canute with the historical follow-on of the Norman Conquest.

The Celts, the Picts and Scots are still to be found in Scotland and Wales but the English came originally to these shores from continental Europe, and the creation of a European Nation meant that we were coming home to be re-embraced into the European Family.

It was a theme which I used repeatedly at scores of meetings throughout the country years after urging our entry into the Common Market, but always stressing that the Common Market was only the first step towards unification.

Economics played little part in Mosley's post-war platform delivery, although he stressed the need for consensus government in the interim stage before achieving the ultimate ideal. The objective of the Corporate State was completely abandoned, on account of its excessive bureaucracy.

He was more concerned with the threat of European domination by Russia, and he stated the historical fact that one European country had withstood the might of the armed forces of the world before final defeat, and he posed the thought of the power and might that could be achieved by three hundred million Europeans as a force for social progress and advancement, and as a buffer state between the two present world powers, thereby presenting the hope of world peace.

Around the time of the launch of Union Movement I was invited to a meeting in a London hotel to be attended by Oswald Mosley. It was packed with familiar faces, many of whom had not been detained, and I had not seen since the spring of 1940. The occasion was so highly charged with emotion that only the coldest blooded human could have failed to be influenced by the atmosphere.

Here was our beloved leader, re-united with his comrades who were straining at the leash to take up the struggle once again, and to march beside him, no matter what the cost. No task was too hard, no goal beyond striving, no price too high.

We passed through the fire, scorched but with unbroken spirit, undaunted, but awaiting the call to carry on from where we had been interrupted those few but interminable years ago. Some of us thought our movement, absolved, like the Labour Party leaders of 1914-18 from the odium of opposition to war, would be given the opportunity to govern.

Mosley, however, soon put an end to such flights of the heart and mind. He made us aware of the great changes that had come about in the economic and industrial atmosphere of post-war Britain. This, combined with the dismembered empire and the changes in the world situation required a complete reappraisal of our own position. New ideas were required to meet the challenge, ideas which he developed before us. He did not minimise the task ahead. It would be another long, hard haul before victory could even be envisaged.

It required great courage and great faith to remain true to the Man after this dashing to the ground of our ill-considered hopes and pipe dreams of glory and early victory, and for some the prospect, and more especially the changes in Movement policy and emphases, proved too much. I never saw Tommy Moran again. Like Frances-Hawkins and a number of other leading pre-war figures, his heart could not fully come to terms with the loss of the Empire ideal forced on us by the disastrous war. Like some others he found himself ten years older than his pre-war heyday, raising the new problems of personal survival in the post-war world. He was active and spoke for a few years in Union Movement but finally left after what I believe was personality problems within the Movement, a situation which he would have handled differently in his prime. His departure was a very sad loss. He was a grand fighter and comrade, of whom O.M. was very fond, and in spite of the circumstances of his going, he will always be remembered for these qualities. He was to die some years later at a comparatively early age.

For me the loss was particularly deep. It was he and that penny

'Blackshirt' who won me for the Movement way back in 1933, and who encouraged me to mount my first public platform in Ormskirk shortly after.

What were my hopes for the Movement in those early post-war years? I was convinced that eventually Mosley would win. Even when the war was over I believed that his new concept of Europe a Nation would carry the people at the end of the day.

I had reckoned without the full impact of the long years of wartime propaganda, however, when the Establishment and its media, together with all our political and other enemies, had had a field day, pouring out the lies and innuendoes without fear of reply.

I found that you could discuss politics and issues with people without mentioning Mosley's name, and gain their sympathetic attention and in many instances approval and support. But once you told them these were the ideas and policies of Oswald Mosley you were cut off dead. It took me many years to realise that we were probably fighting a losing battle.

Policies and circumstances meant that there were appreciable differences between British Union and the post-war Union Movement. Before the war Mosley and the Movement had convictions of achievement. After 1945 it was a hope. There was a mountain to climb and he didn't know whether he would reach the top. I think he anticipated a great surge of enthusiasm, similar to that which had existed before the war, but in the prosperous post-war period, it never really emerged.

In the Blackshirt Movement there was a great feeling of oneness. Mosley always referred to us as 'his Blackshirts', even when the uniform had gone. To his Blackshirts it was a very great honour to belong to an elite that crossed all class barriers. Inevitably this intensity of feeling did not exist in the post-war movement. I myself did not have the same force of inner conviction, and indeed did not play a very active part in Union Movement affairs, though I spoke at some meetings, and contributed occasional articles — for the feature "Small Shopkeeper's Front" for example — in "Union" and "*Action*".

By 1950 it was clear that the Council of Retail Distributors was in decline, a fact which no doubt owed to Beaverbrook's decision to withdraw financial support. Seven years later it was wound up. Long before this, however, my own Chamber of Trade had become affiliated to the increasingly influential National Chamber of Trade and in 1951 I went to my first conference of this body.

I had already attended a number of meetings at area level but was unknown outside the Lancashire - Cheshire - Westmorland areas. I had noticed, during my early years in the field of trade politics, that the majority of people seemed to set great store by a cloak of respectability, but in an endeavour to draw attention to myself I did not wear this cloak, but rather strove to achieve interest in my ideas by brash and provocative behaviour and attitudes. I did not deliberately chase or hog the microphone, but if any arguments were used in support of a resolution which struck me as not being acceptable I would try to be the last speaker from the rostrum and deliver a broadside very often with devastating effect.

Over the years I found that I could often swing the voting on an issue upon which I held a strong viewpoint in favour of my own opinion. I suppose I was becoming a little arrogant, but on the other hand many delegates to meeting and conference would often seek my support on specific subjects.

Sometimes a resolution to conference would be tabled in the name of my own Chamber but I did not always win, and I did learn to be a good loser. After all, I already had many years of practice which had taught me not to be too despondent when I lost.

I found that I was enjoying this kind of life, but to make it possible, business had to be profitable, and we were now nearing the period of price cutting and special offers, together with the unfair policy of 'loss leaders', adopted by the newly emerging supermarkets.

In 1952, I was elected President of my Chamber and this added to my prestige at both area and national level. I was now more knowledgeable in matters concerning the whole field of distribution, and this stimulated my long-time interest in Parliamentary affairs, particularly when legislation was being introduced into the parliamentary calendar which might have a damaging effect upon the survival of small businessmen.

The eventual lifting of all rationing restrictions and the gradual improvement in the availability of consumer goods had seen the emergence of the early supermarkets, and I was quick to appreciate the challenge which they would soon make for dominance of the retail market.

I sought every opportunity to press my arguments in favour of some form of protection for the smaller concern, not only from the standpoint of self-preservation, but because the use of 'loss leaders' by the bigger stores would make for unfair competition. In the long-term I argued the housewife would be the ultimate loser when the small independent business had been driven into bankruptcy and monopoly conditions dictated the ultimate retail level of prices.

I confess that in the early stages of my campaign I made few converts. Rather was I looked upon as a prophet of doom who was afraid of the competitive market and sought protection against the more efficient style of large store special offers and impulse buying. It would be many years before the rapidly increasing numbers of failed business in the food section of retailing finally forced an acceptance of my early forecasts.

Following a recommendation by the first post-war Parliamentary Boundary Commission, the University Seats were abolished, and Sir Arthur Salter, an economic adviser to Winston Churchill, lost his Oxford seat, and Churchill sought a safe seat for his return to Parliament.

When Harold Wilson abandoned the marginal Labour seat of Ormskirk it was recaptured for the Tories by Sir Ronald Cross. I met the new member on a number of occasions, and found him a likeable and fascinating conversationalist.

On more than one occasion he tried to persuade me to join the Conservative Party, with the long-term view of seeking Parliamentary honours. As a follow-up to this suggestion I was unexpectedly invited to the home of the treasurer of the Ormskirk Conservative Party for an evening, and somewhat intrigued, I accepted. He was a man well-known in Burscough as an influential member of his party, and I waited the occasion with some interest.

The treasurer told me he was fully aware of my Mosley association even hinting that he had been a sympathiser, but Mosley's hopes for a political revival, he said, were nil. If I had political ambitions he could help to realise them. He offered me the chairmanship of the Burscough and Latham Branch of the Ormskirk Conservative Party, assuring me of his sponsorship if I chose to seek parliamentary recognition.

After a few days of thought I accepted his offer. I told myself that Mosley had been a member of both the Conservative and the Labour Parties before forming his own, and that I might be able to further his cause through less obvious channels. It was not an easy decision to make, and I felt that for the first time since the awakening of my political conscience I was being insincere.

Not long after Ronald Cross was made Governor General of Tasmania, and Sir Arthur Salter was returned in his place as the

Ormskirk member. At the following General Election we had another change owing to Salter's elevation to the Lords, and our new member was Sir Douglas Glover. I even helped him in his election campaign, acting as opening speaker on a number of occasions, but was never really at home.

I felt I was a fraud, and talking with my 'tongue in my cheek', but I persevered in the hope that a calmer mind would emerge. I frequently met Douglas Glover at his fortnightly surgery in the town, and he was an indefatigable champion of free enterprise.

When the time came round for the election to the local Council I accepted an invitation to contest one of the three

Burscough and Latham wards. This, the one in which I lived, was so strongly Labour that it had not been contested since the early 1930's.

I put up a reasonable fight, captured 40% of the vote, and was quite satisfied with the result. My local sponsor then suggested that it was time for me to make my bid for acceptance as a prospective Parliamentary candidate, and for this I required two MP sponsors. Sir Douglas Glover readily agreed, and for my second sponsor I approached Colonel Hesketh, of Meols Hall, the MP for Southport who I knew from my tenancy days of his cottage in Churchtown. He seemed surprised at my approach, but my knowledge of politics and economics seemed to impress him, that he said he thought I might be an acquisition to Westminster.

My next hurdle was to get approval from the area office in Manchester, and I must have passed muster here because they arranged for me to go down to Conservative Party Central Office in London.

There, the interviewing Panel was made up of three senior officials, including the .Chairman of the party. I was first asked why I wanted to be a parliamentary candidate to which I replied that for many years I had had political ambitions, that my experience in a co-operative bakery had dispelled any socialist dreams I may have nurtured in my youth, that I was a firm believer in personal initiative and private enterprise, that I had a good grounding in economic theory, and that my ability as a platform speaker and debater should make me a good candidate.

I was then asked to recount my previous political experiences, which I did informing them of my earlier nomination as prospective B.U.F. parliamentary candidate for East Hull.

I made no attempt to minimise the extent of my pre-war political involvement, and, with some cynical anticipation, awaited their reaction. I was asked if I did not consider that my earlier commitment might be a deterrent against my acceptance, to which I replied that Winston Churchill started his career as a Conservative, but first entered Parliament as a Liberal, and later changed his coat again to the Conservative colour and eventually became Prime Minister. I conceded that I was a career Conservative but argued that this could not impede me since it was generally admitted that the majority of Liberal and Conservative MPs were also career politicians. The interview lasted about an hour, and I was thanked for my attendance, and for my honesty which was appreciated.

I made one further attempt to seek election to the local Council. I was still chairman of the local branch and had been chosen to fight the customary Conservative seat, after having declined to oppose the sitting member, Counsellor Jackie Dawson, a Labour man who was seeking re-election in the ward I had fought the previous year.

My reasons were quite logical. Not only was Jackie a personal friend, he was also a good man at the job and I had no wish to displace him even if that had been possible, which I doubted. The seat I was to contest was 'up for grabs', since the retiring member did not wish to continue. Unfortunately, we were only a branch of the constituency party, and our decisions had to be approved by Central Office which asked for nominations. Two other names were submitted, one being the choice of an influential member of the central committee. Neither of the alternative nominees lived in the area, but the final choice pushed me out in favour of an Ormskirk resident, subsequently elected.

This small example of inside jiggery-pokery to prevent the election of a one-time Blackshirt rather dismayed me, and at the first suitable opportunity I withdrew from local politics. In later years I was approached to re-enter the field, and virtually guaranteed a safe seat, but I had already had a surfeit of behind-the-scenes chicanery, and that put an end to my political ambitions. I heard nothing further from Central Office about my adoption as a prospective Parliamentary candidate, but that must have been a dead duck from the start.

I had known Wilfred Edge for a number of years and had worked closely alongside him during my period with the Committee for the Employment of Disabled Persons. An elderly man, and a long-standing business figure in Burscough, he called in to the shop one day to talk to me. To my surprise he asked me if I would be willing to serve on the local Magistrates Bench, of which he had been Chairman for a number of years. I felt highly honoured, and readily stated my willingness to serve as a JP. It was considered a far greater honour in the 1950's than it is today.

I filled in the questionnaire sent to all nominees, and returned it to the appropriate department. Mr. Edge had submitted numerous names for appointment to the Bench during his time and he confidently awaited the result so that he could compliment me on appointment. No such appointment, however, was made. The questionnaire was very searching in its range of queries, and I had been quite honest in my answers. Some months later Mr. Edge informed me that in all his years as a Magistrate he had not previously proposed a candidate who had not been appointed and he had no idea as to the possible reason. He was quite apologetic, but I assured him that I probably knew the answer. He asked me if I had ever been sentenced to a term of imprisonment, I answered no, but I had spent most of the war detained in prisons and concentration camps as a Mosley Blackshirt. He looked at me with deep concern, and then said: "I am sorry", but he did not say exactly why he was sorry. I like to think that it was because he regretted the bias which had denied me the honour, not that he regretted my Mosley affiliation. It could have been a little of both. We remained good friends until his death a few years ago.

By now my trade association commitments were: the South West Lancashire Chamber of Trade, whose area and national delegate I was; the Southport Master Bakers, which required attendance at area and national meetings, as well as on the area wage negotiating committee; the Southport Chamber of Trade; and the Southport Grocers Federation, which also held area and national meetings. I was almost fully committed since I was still working full-time in my bakery, but I could not have coped with one-half of these demands on my time without the loyal and constant help of my wife.

I had not expected to further broaden my scope of activity but my Chamber was asked to submit a name for service on the local NHSS Tribunals, and since the tribunals were always held in Southport, and in the afternoon, I allowed my name to go forward for appointment. I am glad that I did, because it led to a period of public service which I greatly enjoyed.

The tribunal is composed of three people: a worker representative, usually from the local branch of a trade union; a representative from the employers, very often from a Chamber of Trade; and an independent chairman, who was a solicitor. I served under three chairmen, the first Alderman Charles Aveling of Southport, who I had known for a number of years through his membership of the Board of Management of the National Chamber of Trade. He was a well-loved figure at our annual conferences, and when I attended my first tribunal he gave me a very warm welcome. I had little to say at my first attendance but later took an active part in the cases which were widely divergent in character. All aspects of payment from the NHSS can be subject to the decisions of an official of the department, but all claimants, irrespective of the reasons given by the Insurance Officer, can be challenged.

Shortly before Alderman Aveling's retirement he asked me if I would allow him to nominate me for appointment to the Magistrates bench. I told him I had no objection but that I considered that he would be wasting his time. He looked rather surprised, but when I explained what had happened on the last occasion when my name was put forward, he agreed that it would be futile exercise. He did, however, say that he was not in agreement with my failure to make the grade, and expressed his regret.

I continued to serve on the tribunals until 1984, and after such a long period of unbroken service I was curious as to the form the appreciation from official quarters would take. There was no recognition at all, and I was not even officially informed that my services were terminated. It was when I arrived to sit on a tribunal that I was told by the clerk that I would not be called upon again. The local department had received notification that I had completed my present term and would not be reappointed.

Not even an official notice of termination, or even a letter of thanks. I did receive a letter from the chairman expressing his personal thanks, and his regret that I was not to be reappointed.

The years now seemed to fly. I had so many commitments that a journalist writing for the Baker's Review in a pen-picture of me used as a banner headlines, the well known quotation: "He has not time to Stand and Stare", which I must confess at the time gave me no little gratification. Attending annual conferences regularly, I was a contributor to many discussions on the trade problems of the day, some of which included the old British Union policy of protection for Lancashire textiles, as well as a clarification on ownership in relation to a motor vehicle log book, and a call for the nationalised industries be made responsible to Parliament.

I enjoyed the annual conference, but soon realised that if I was to influence policy at national level it would be necessary to seek election to the board of management.

There were two methods of election to the Board. One was through the area councils as an area representative, the other was by election at the annual conference as a national representative, and this was what I wanted. I had already built up some measure of support from the floor of the conference and I thought that I could turn this to my advantage, but I reckoned without the complexities of the human character.

Every organisation builds up within itself the concept of 'them and us', or the inbuilt suspicion that once you create a governing body, it will not always represent the general view. I had not appreciated that in the main my support from the floor of the conference arose from the conviction that I was one of the crowd, who could be expected to champion its cause against the authoritative elite.

Standing for election to the board I was devastated to find that I was at the bottom of the poll. It was no consolation to be told by scores of delegates afterwards that they had not voted for me because they wanted me, as "one of them", to continue on the floor of the conference, not on the platform. It was a lesson well learned.

In my first five years of National Chamber involvement, one man stands out as unique, Arthur McTaggart Short, shortly to become national President of the Chamber, a Welshman born in Cardiff with a Scottish name. He was a gregarious extrovert whose natural ebullience endeared him to me long before he became a close associate and friend. Words flowed from his tongue like a silver cascade of sparkling spring water, dappled with scintillating effusion of dazzling hyperbole.

His ability to conjure words clothed in the magic of descriptive prose almost made me envious. I thought I had a good command of the English language but he left me at the starting line when it came to linguistic erudition. In his presidential address he used as a motif the Latin phrase: 'Sursum Corda' from the Tridentine Mass, which means 'Lift up your Heart'. I awaited a suitable opportunity of going to the speaker's rostrum. At the conclusion of my comments I referred to and quoted his admonition to the delegates and replied, after turning and looking directly at him, "Habemus Spiritum Tecum". I turned and looked at him again and I knew from the twinkle in his eye that he had understood my crude Latin translation.

In 1951, the Mosley's moved from their home in Wiltshire to take up residence in the Republic of Ireland. Although Union Movement had been launched in early 1948, the anticipated programme of meetings and street marches had been severely hit by the almost total ban on the hiring of public halls and the Home Office's similar ban on street demonstrations in East London. The animosity of the postwar Labour Government towards Oswald Mosley and the new Movement, and its determination to retard its growth, was quite remarkable.

After three years however, there were mounting pressures within the Movement to renew the initiative for a series of meetings in the major towns and cities of Britain, and through it, build up mass support for our policies. I was very encouraged to receive an invitation to spend a weekend of discussion in Dublin with OM, together with Raven Thomson, the Movement's number two, and Bob Row.

I was elated to think that my opinion was considered worthy

of consideration, and so, accompanied by Edith, I left by an early flight from Speke airport in a mood of keen anticipation. Neither of us had been to Ireland before, though I had known many Irishmen within the ranks of our Movement. We wandered around Dublin in the afternoon, and dined with Mosley later that evening. We were staying at the same hotel, and after Edith retired to bed, OM and I continued our discussions into the early hours.

The following afternoon and evening we discussed the political climate and kindred subjects. I agreed to test the opinion and views of pre- and post-war members regarding the amount of interest that might be expected from a series of public meetings.

Although I did not deliberately introduce the subject of Mosley and his policies among my Chamber of Trade associates I had never attempted to hide my views and was on occasion given opportunities to discuss them. Their reception was seldom antagonistic. Raven Thomson was to provide me with the addresses of all known supporters in the Manchester area and I would convene a meeting in the city.

Shortly afterwards I told Stanley Hull that I was seeking a suitable venue for a private meeting in Manchester, and asked if he could recommend one. He inquired what kind of meeting it was, and as he was already aware of my political connections I told him that Oswald Mosley would be the speaker, but that it would be restricted to supporters of the idea of a United Europe.

He advised me to approach the Midland Hotel as the least likely to refuse. This I did, and had no difficulty in booking a large room on the ground floor. The meeting was very well attended and I was pleased to see present pre-war East London's Mick Clarke. As far as I know it was the only major post-war meeting that Mick attended, although I am told he did speak at an open air meeting in Derby in the early 50's.

I never heard of him again which made me sad, because he had been special in our Movement. As a very young man he had been one of the four founder members of London's East End N/E Bethnal Green Branch which by 1939 had grown under his influence to a four figure membership. He was a first class speaker with a style of his own, which almost gave him the kind of charisma which Mosley always exuded. By 1939, he had become Propaganda Administrator at National Headquarters and was one of the 'top five' who signed Mosley's Message to Members on the outbreak of war.

Mick's first marriage broke up whilst he was detained and I believe underwent much hardship after the war in finding employment. He ultimately re-married and lived in the North for many years and I have recently been informed that he is alive and fit. There is one thing of which I am certain, that is wherever he is, Mick Clarke, even in age, will not have forgotten those glorious days we of British Union shared together in the fight for a Greater Britain.

In the early 50's Mosley advocated syndicalism or workers ownership as the third force in contrast to the bureaucratic state control of Socialism and Communism on one side and free for all Capitalism on the other. In time this gave way to the less rigid "wage-price mechanism" which he elaborated in a number of books including "Europe Faith and Plan" and his autobiography "My Life".

He also proposed changes in the taxation system, shifting the emphasis from earnings to expenditure in an attempt to encourage effort, responsibility and thrift. Together with Bob Row of Union Movement headquarters (still Editor of "*Action*' after some 30 years) and West Country farmer Bob Saunders, a leading member of the National Farmers Union, I participated in discussion, but the tax change, linked to savings in industrial bonds and government stocks, never became Union Movement policy.

It was around this time that my attendance at a South Coast conference of the National Chamber of Trade coincided with a Union Movement London Country Council election campaign. Oswald Mosley was billed to speak in support of the candidates on the day scheduled for my return, and I was asked if I would be available to take up the role of opening speaker. This I readily agreed to do.

The meeting was well attended and as usual, orderly. I had been speaking for nearly half an hour when I saw Mosley at the rear of the half. He intimated that I was to carry on, which I did for a time until it was appropriate to invite him to the platform. Until this moment few people knew he had arrived, and so my words fitted the occasion admirably. I remained on the platform to greet him, and he gave me that customary look that always revitalised my spirits, going on to address the large audience in his usual inimitable style.

Not long after, one of our open-air meetings was scheduled for Trafalgar Square, and again was asked if I would be opening speaker. I had attended a number of Trafalgar Square meetings before the war but this was the first time that I had been given the opportunity of speaking from the plinth of Nelson's Column.I took my son and one of his school friends with me this time and we went down by car.

It was the largest meeting I have ever addressed, and it still lives in my memory as a very special occasion. After all, there are many prominent politicians who will never speak in Trafalgar Square, and I was quite proud of my presence there.

It was a crowd of many thousands, and apart from a little barracking, quite orderly. No doubt many of the crowd were Mosley supporters and even those who were not gave him loud applause many times.

When he appeared on the outskirts of the crowd I could no longer

The author, wartime detention behind him, takes time off to open a meeting for Mosley in East London in 1949 where the new Union Movement was contesting the LCC elections.

retain the crowd's attention and I just stood silent, awaiting his arrival. He thanked me most warmly for 'holding the fort', and I was again a spellbound listener. It was the only time my son ever saw him or heard him speak.

About the time of the Suez crisis in 1956 I was asked to become president of the Southport Grocers Federation, and through this position, an executive member of the town's Chamber of Trade. Since I was also president of both the Bakers and Grocers Association, my diary, and that of Edith, was becoming rather heavy!

During this period I met Edward du Cann, then a Minister in the MacMillan Government. He had been invited to address the Chamber of Trade conference of that year and struck me as being a very forceful speaker with a promising Parliamentary career. Du Cann had already made a name for himself in the City as a budding property entrepreneur, and the lunch break in proceedings enabled me to talk to him in greater detail on

various economic aspects of Government policy. His close associate at Lonrho, Tiny Rowland, was also beginning to emerge
as a future tycoon and I was tempted to introduce his name, but
decided against it. I had not seen Tiny Rowland since Peel Camp
in 1942.

In our conversation I did admit that I did at one time have
parliamentary ambitions but the war intervened and put paid to
them. He looked at me with the faint glimmerings of a smile but
made no further comment. I was surprised when he limited his
parliamentary career to Chairmanship of the 1922 Committee.
I had thought of him as a probable occupant of No. 10, but his
unconventional city career almost certainly acted as a brake.

We were now in the period of continued argument over entry
into the Common Market and it was only to be expected as a
dedicated European I automatically campaigned for Britain's
entry.

There was still much opposition to direct European involvement
throughout the country, and I found myself in great demand as a
supporting speaker from a wide variety of organisations.

I travelled many thousands of miles in my endeavours to
encourage support for our entry, accepting invitations from local
branches of The Women's Institute, the Housewives League,
the Business and Professional Women's Organisation, Rotary
Clubs, and meetings of The Inner Wheel. I covered the whole
of the Northern counties and travelled as far as Leicester and
Chesterfield, as well as many Chamber of Trade meetings in
numerous towns. In the National Chamber I became known as
a willing exponent of Common Market commitments and rarely
refused an invitation to speak.

One meeting stands out in particular, because of the comments
of a woman in Rochdale. It was a meeting of the Townswomen's
Guild, with a large and attentive audience. At the conclusion of

the meeting I was approached by an elderly, well-spoken lady.

After complimenting me on my address, she made particular reference to my style of delivery and the fact that I never used notes or read from a prepared script. She told me that in all her experience she had only met one person who was a better speaker, and that I was very similar to him in style, with the constant use of gestures and the rise and fall of voice volume.

She was surprised when I told her that she must be speaking of my friend Oswald Mosley. Smiling she said she had heard him speak in Rochdale Town Hall in 1934. She was even more surprised when I told her that I had been present at that meeting.

Between 1953 and 1959, Union Movement published "The European", a quite outstanding monthly magazine devoted to politics, literature and the arts. In an early issue, Oswald Mosley wrote an article under the title, "A Question of Faith", to which I replied in some detail.

"There is no doubt that the faith of the German people under the Third Reich sublimated in belief in The Fuhrer, which during the war years produced almost superhuman achievements until they finally succumbed to attack from all sides", I wrote.

"Why was this faith in the early years so unacceptable to the democracies? No one has provided a logical reason for the bitter hatred of National Socialism when compared to the much milder antagonism towards Mussolini's Fascism, Salazar's National Syndicalism, and Spain's Francoism. The war between Italy and Abyssinia did not produce one per cent of the hatred engendered by the reoccupation of the Rhineland by German troops. This first act by Hitler produced an immediate response by the British Prime Minister when Baldwin declared in the House that "Our Frontiers are on the Rhine". This outburst by Baldwin should have caused a storm of protest but it met almost universal parliamentary approval.

"No government can prosecute a successful war unless there is hatred against the enemy and it was we who declared war on Germany, not Germany upon us. There was no hatred against this country in Germany before the war and according to some sources very little after the war although we were the victors. How then do we account for this blood-bath when the necessary hatred was so one-sided? The 'despair of soul' which possessed me during the war years compelled me to seek the flaw in Nazi philosophy, and instead of a philosophy there was only concern for material needs of the body, and none for the needs of the spirit.

"The concept of 'Man as God Becoming', and the acceptance of the theory of racial purity antagonised the Christian Church even to an ever-widening rift between the Vatican and the Wilhemstrasse.

"Even a staunch Germanophile like the Swedish explorer and lecturer Sven Hedin looked, with alarm at the anti-Christian trend of the National Socialist State, and is on record as having voiced his concern with many of the Leaders of the Third Reich. Could it be that herein lies the clue to the Hitler experiment?

"Like his predecessor Napoleon he almost succeeded in his military conquests, but unlike Napoleon, his political ideology died with him. In his article Mosley also refers to Napoleon, the French Revolution, and nineteenth century Liberalism, and I more than welcome his view that all who hold spiritual values should work together in the fight against communism. The French revolution eventually gave us democracy but in its early days it was basically materialistic in outlook, and it was Leo 13th in his encyclical The Workers Charter which provided the spiritual background that enabled it to weather the storms of industrial strife for 150 years.

"It would appear to me, then, that unless Mosley's 'Alternative' is clothed in a spiritual package it will not be accepted by the masses, and Europe will be doomed and annihilated under the advancing hordes of Asiatic Bolshevism".

The above was written over 35 years ago and the second political disappointment of my life is the glaring fact that despite the Common Market, European Unity is no nearer today than it was when Mosley first enunciated the concept in 1948. It took the tragedy and aftermath of the Second World War to create the Common Market. Will it require an even greater conflict to bring into being 'Europe a Nation'?

In 1960 I made my first television appearance as a spokesman for the small independent trader. It was a confrontational type of interview on one of the early presentations screened by a northern television company operating from a small studio in Manchester, A.B.C. at Large, and the interviewer was Desmond Wilcox.

My opponent was a director of the rapidly expanding supermarket chain to Tesco, and the subject, the merits and demerits of supermarket trading versus the small trader from the stand point of the housewife. My argument was that in the initial stage, the supermarket through its bulk purchasing power would be able to buy cheaper and it thus could offer 'loss leaders' (items deliberately sold at less than cost), and still remain a profitable exercise. In the long term, however, when years of undercutting by the supermarket had driven most of the smaller units into bankruptcy, monopoly conditions would emerge with the larger distributor dictating price to the manufacturer and housewife. When monopoly conditions prevail, competition disappears, and the housewife would eventually mourn the loss of the private shop.

I have always been able to banish into the deep subconscious, events or happenings with an unhappy connotation, and when they emerge I usually quickly concentrate my thoughts on other matters.

Early in March 1958, Edith became pregnant. It was unexpected but not unwelcome. Our daughter was twenty-four and our son was just eighteen, and we were rather hesitant to inform them of the situation. We thought they might be embarrassed, but far from it. I told them during a meal and cannot forget the comment of my son. He was sitting opposite to me at the table and he looked up at me and with a twinkle in his eye said, "I'll bet you're proud of yourself, Dad". So much for the announcement!

The birth was quite normal and in November Edith presented me with a most beautiful baby girl with black curly hair and the darkest eyes I have ever seen. She died a few days later. Medical science would save her today, but 30 years ago the techniques for operations at such an early age were not available. I won't say any more. It was a traumatic time particularly for Edith. I was able to cram my life with other interests and so avoid dwelling on the loss.

As the short Eden years merged into the Indian Summer of Harold MacMillan, there was one aspect of Union Movement's policy which I thought had some immediate potential for political advancement; mass coloured immigration.

Travelling the country a great deal, I knew that the vast majority of British people were opposed to the creation of a multi-racial society. Union Movement had opposed coloured immigration since 1952. As Jeffrey Hamm, general secretary of the Movement in the late '50s and '60s, and now secretary of *Action Society* succinctly puts it, "We said it all and we said it first".

The Movement's far-sighted and always principled policy on immigration was denounced by the old parties and their media as "race hatred". Others did indeed peddle hatred, but Mosley and Union Movement never attacked the immigrant, but rather those in authority in this country who ruined the Caribbean economies and then brought West Indians over here in large and increasing numbers to our northern island.

The author then Chairman of his local Conservatives with his wife Edith and good friend Labour Councillor Jackie Dawson, Chairman of Ormskirk U.D. Council, and wife Chrissie at the Chairman's Ball in the 1950's.

Mosley stood as Union Movement Parliamentary candidate for North Kensington — which included the Notting Hill area — in the General Election of October 1959. I went along to his adoption meeting which was wildly enthusiastic. I remember there were quite a number of coloured people present, and they were also wildly enthusiastic, no doubt because for the first time they were hearing an English politician talking about giving black people a square deal — in their own countries. There was absolutely no racial antagonism at this meeting, a point worth stressing in view of the slanders of our opponents.

In contrast to many Union Movement members and supporters, I didn't expect Mosley to win, but his recorded vote of just under 3,000 was a shock to us all and the greatest disappointment of my life.

Mosley and the Movement had fought a magnificent campaign amid every sign of great popularity and enthusiasm. If even a large proportion of voting pledges had been adhered to, we would have won the day. There were electoral irregularities, including missing ballot boxes, but nothing could be changed.

Despite this disappointment however, Union Movement reached its greatest vigour and strength in the early sixties, until organised violence by Communists and Jewish elements at open air meetings in the summer of 1962 — accompanied needless to say by a thoroughly dishonest Press coverage and the old enmity of the Establishment — put a brake on the activities of a Movement led by a man in his 66th year.

But as with the lost peace of 1939/40 we can say, what a national disaster, what miseries and tragic errors would have been avoided if the sane, rational and humane immigration policies of Mosley and Union Movement had been implemented in the 1950s!

It was in 1962 that I was elected chairman of the North West Area Council of the National Chamber. With a territory extending from the Wirral and Cheshire to the Scottish border, and bounded on the east by the Pennines, demands on my time increased enormously.

With Britain still in the throes of the Common Market debate, the secretary of the Bolton Chamber, Bernard Tennant arranged a debate between myself and James McMillan, one of the principal leader writers of the fervently anti-Common Market "Daily Express".

As well as being a leading journalist, McMillan had a reputation as a platform speaker, and the debate in one of the leading Bolton hotels attracted a good audience.

I also had a reputation as a forceful speaker, particularly if the subject was one on which I held strong views. Then as now, people were widely divided on the issue but my support for the Common Market was based on my concept of a United Europe, and whenever I spoke on the Common Market issue I was also pressing my political view without any direct reference to Mosley's Union Movement. Bernard of course was aware of my political loyalties, though I am not suggesting that he was in any way favourably inclined. He probably was not, but that did not in any way mar our friendship which has prospered with the years. James McMillan was a worthy opponent, well versed in his argument and pulling no punches. He was the best debating opponent I had had in many years. The meeting lasted two-and-a-half hours and at the final vote I lost by a narrow majority.

The debate attracted a good deal of attention in the local press, and a re-run was suggested. This took place in Church House, Ormskirk, the largest available hall in the town, and was packed, with many standing at the rear.

I thought McMillan gave an ever better delivery than in Bolton, but so did I! I felt I was carrying my audience with me, something quickly apparent to any competent speaker. In my peroration I pressed for the kill and carried the day with a narrow majority.

For a number of years Cyril Lord had been a household name in the carpeting field, and it was suggested to me that in view of his infrequent but openly expressed pro-European political opinions I might be able to arrange a meeting between him and Mosley.

Cyril Lord readily agreed to meet me for a talk on the commercial aspects of European Union in his London offices, and I floated the idea of a possible meeting with Oswald Mosley. Unfortunately it was about this time that his carpet empire began to show signs of instability and he was hesitant to commit himself to a firm date.

I was surprised to find that he was even shorter in height than myself, but an absolute dynamo of energy, with bright eyes of indeterminate colour, his conversation liberally adorned with gestures but expressing deep concern and genuine conviction on matters which interested him. He did not strike me as being politically-minded, but his knowledge of commerce and the intricacies of international trade made conversation with him of absorbing interest. I wish I could record that my attempts at arranging a meeting between him and Mosley had been successful, but in this venture I failed. He showed initial interest but I think that his own internal problems demanded his full attention.

In the following eighteen years of my close association with the National Chamber at board of management level; four men stand out as being of special significance aside from Arthur MacTaggart Short. The wisest of these without doubt was Jon Oliver Watkins of Swansea, who guided the financial fortunes of the Chamber for many years as National Treasurer, and was also an outstanding National President. I well recall the time he gave me encouragement when I was most in need.

Another was Charles Dodd, who in his capacity as a solicitor, helped and advised on the numerous occasions when Parliamentary legislation affecting the smaller type of business was being debated on the floor of The House.

The one with the greatest intellect, and in whose judgment I placed great faith, was John Mortlock, an accountant who had made a special study of Common Market Law, and taxation. He was perhaps the most knowledgeable man in the country on V.A.T., and often in direct consultation with Customs and Excise before the introduction of this tax into the United Kingdom.

Finally there is Les Seeney, now Director General of the National Chamber and perhaps the one most closely involved with my own activities at national level.

It is interesting to note that all four received the O.B.E. for their services to the field of distribution and all were richly deserving of the honour. For me to make recognition of their services is perhaps a measure of the regard in which I hold them, since I am not noted for fulsome praise, or the paying of undeserved compliments.

The first time I became directly involved was when Ted Heath, then Minister at the Board of Trade, was introducing his Bill for the abandonment of Retail Price Maintenance. A protest meeting was organised by the National Chamber at St. Pancras Town Hall, packed to the doors with delegates from all over the country, the first of a national series. The meeting received wide publicity and my own contribution from the floor received tumultuous support from the assembled delegates. I even remember my opening clarion call: "Cry Havoc!, Let Loose the Dogs of War". I was asked to join the platform for meetings in St. George's Hall, Liverpool, and a Glasgow meeting, where my scathing remarks about Ted Heath were greeted with great gusto. We lost that battle, and since then have had the fiasco of the Sunday Trading Bill.

For months past I had been reading articles in the Chamber of Trade monthly Journal by a W.J. Leaper. I had known a W.J. Leaper before the war but had no way of knowing if this was the same person. Then I was presented with an opportunity of talking to him at the conference social function. He too was a member of the board, and as we chatted at the bar, I was unable to deduce if we had previously met, so I asked him if he had pre-war journalistic experience. My reason for asking was because the Leaper I had known in the mid '30's had been the editor of the 'Blackshirt', one of the weekly newspapers of the Movement.

He looked at me rather quizzically and said yes. I then asked him if he had been associated with a political weekly and if its colour had been black. He answered yes, from then on we started to exchange memories of the past. He was the only one of the pre-war Movement that I ever spoke to on these lines within the National Chamber of Trade. I knew there were many old British Union supporters but for a variety of reasons they chose not to disclose it to me, though most of them knew that I was aware of their old allegiance.

I had to admit that it could be to your disadvantage in business to be known as an ex-Blackshirt, and many were concerned lest their children suffer opprobrium as a result. I always respected their wishes. Bill Leaper openly accepted his past and never asked me to remain silent, though this is the first time I have ever referred to it.

The trade press had been showing renewed interest in the Retail Price Maintenance issue and I had taken up the cudgels on behalf of the small trader when the trade weekly 'The Grocer' abandoned the fight for the maintenance of R.P.M. I attacked them for what I termed their 'stab in the back', and as a follow up I was invited to express my views on television, my opposite number again being the director from Tesco's.

The programme went out 'live', and when I got home Edith told me there had been a number of 'phone calls about the programme. The next time the 'phone rang I answered it and the caller asked if I was the John Charnley who, before the war, had lived in Hull. He had been a Hull Blackshirt now living in North Wales. We chattered for a while, and two further calls turned out to be old Blackshirts who had recognised me.

It was about this time that I was chased by the national Press. They thought they had dropped on to a good story. It was at the time of the emergence of the minor French politician Pierre Poujade in his organised campaign of tax rebellion by the French shopkeepers. I had been at a meeting of the North West Federation of Master Bakers and in exasperation against some proposed government restriction had said I was tempted to take a leaf out of Poujade's book. The Press took this to mean that I was going to start my own party, and I was hard put to convince them otherwise.

My multifarious activities continued for many years, but from 1972, with my retirement from business, I began a slow withdrawal from a strenuous life to trade politics.

Among the highlights of this period were trade missions to France in 1969 and Germany in 1973, and the chairmanship of the Committee of inquiry into the running of the National Chamber.

In 1972 I sold my Burscough Bridge business, and, not without some stretching of our resources, bought a small property block in Churchtown, Southport, in part of which we now live. During these more relaxed years Edith and I have been able to make four trips to Australia to visit our son and his family. Golden days!

For a long time the National Chamber of Trade has received two invitations each year to attend one of the Royal garden parties at Buckingham Palace. It is usual for one invitation to be given to the National President and the other to a member of the board of management.

The invitations normally include immediate members of the recipient's family, and Edith and Rose were more than delighted when the invitation arrived from the Lord Chancellor's office.

It was a day to be remembered. We met National President Len Turner, for lunch before making our way to the Palace. It had rained heavily all morning but when we made our approach down the Mall the clouds suddenly cleared, the sun shone as we finally walked through the Palace gates.

It was quite an experience to walk unhindered around the grounds after having passed through the Palace itself, and was surprised to bump into Enoch Powell, who I had met a few months earlier at a Conservative dinner in Ormskirk. He was there as guest speaker, and I had chatted with him later in the evening. He was already notorious for his attitude to coloured immigration and I wanted to challenge him on his earlier attitude, when as Minister of Health, he had encouraged the influx of Afro-Caribbeans into the National Health Service. However this was to be a day of pleasurable enjoyment, so I refrained.

I was surprised to see how small the Queen is in stature, but what a flawless complexion and how natural her demeanour. She was in truth a Princess and a Queen. That day was one of the most enjoyable I have spent in my life, all the more so because I had never anticipated such an occasion coming my way, and more particularly because of the joy it gave my wife.

I have not been the easiest of persons to live with and to know that this undoubted pleasure came as a result of my endeavours in a sphere completely divorced from my earlier commitments, was in some small measure a repayment, even if only in part, for what has often meant anxiety and worry.

In the late 'seventies, while occupying the secretaryship of the two adjoining Chambers of Formby and Crosby, I was approached by BBC Radio to take part in a broadcast on the "Battle of Olympia" of 1934.

My contribution was based on my part as a Blackshirt steward and was recorded from the studios of Radio Merseyside. Other participants included a police inspector, two Communists who had also been present, and two left wing intellectuals who later became well-known Labour MPs.

The programme went out at 7pm the following Monday, which was unfortunate because I had to attend a South West Lancashire Chamber committee meeting. I arrived having given little thought to the programme, and was having a pre-meeting drink at the bar when I was joined by a fellow committee member.

With a subtle chuckle he told me that just before coming out he had been listening to Radio 4. He wanted to know if he had recognised the voice of one of the contributors, because though he had not been listening to the announcer, he was fairly certain that he had recognised my voice. I told him that he was correct, and that I had made the recording a few days earlier in the Liverpool studio. He complimented me on my presentation, and said that he had been told that I was a pre-war Blackshirt, and asked if I still supported the same views. When I told him that I did, he showed quite a fair amount of interest.

More distant recollections surfaced one day while I was serving a customer at Scotts of Ormskirk where I was a business associate. After observing me rather closely a woman asked if I had ever addressed meetings in Ormskirk. Assuming that she was referring to my Chamber of Trade activities I acknowledged my involvement.

Looking puzzled, she said she was thinking of before the war and political meetings on the corner of Moor Street. I complimented her on her memory. "Yes", she replied, "my brother joined your Movement. He often spoke of you after you moved to Yorkshire, and I used to go with him to your open-air meetings. You've altered very little apart from the colour of your hair." Her brother had died during the war.

On another occasion a customer asked me if I had lived in Scarisbrick Street, Southport before the war. She reminded me that I used to buy cigarettes from her shop there, and was nearly always dressed in the Blackshirt uniform. I also recall meeting a senior official of a nationalised industry who told me I had signed him up as a British Union member after one of my Ormskirk meetings.

With regular Chamber meetings in London and my own local work in South West Lancashire, I was advised by my doctor in 1982 to cut back on my work load. My term of office on the National Chamber board of management would expire at the annual conference in May, and I had already decided I would not stand for re-election, although I was being pressured to serve for another three years.

South West Lancashire showed their generous appreciation of my work in the form of a cut-glass decanter and some beautiful claret glasses. The National Chamber conference was being held in Guernsey, and as usual was preceded by a pre-conference meeting of the Board on which I had served for 18 years.

I attended the meeting with mixed feelings. I appreciated that I was not as fit as I used to be, and though I did not regret my decision not to stand for re-election, I was feeling somewhat subdued with the knowledge that this was to be the end of a very active thirty-five years in chamber affairs. When the item of elections to the Board was raised it was quite casually mentioned that a vacancy had occurred due to the retirement of Mr. Charnley who did not intend to stand for re-election. I waited in anticipation for what might follow ... and nothing did. Not a word of thanks, not a single congratulatory comment or word of appreciation on tasks accomplished. I would have been somewhat embarrassed to have received one. But to be ignored, allowed to pass out without comment seemed extraordinary. But perhaps I was mistaken, perhaps there would be some word of recognition during the conference sessions, or at some social function?

It was not to be. The end was indeed the end. Not a word from anybody. Awaiting a taxi to take us to the airport, I told Len Turner how I felt. Later I received a letter from the National President and one from the Director-General expressing regret at the apparently cavalier fashion in which my retirement had been passed over.

The subsequent thanks which came a year later at the Buxton conference together with the accolade of Honorary Vice President of the National Chamber left me quite cold. I felt that if I had not expressed my feelings to Len Turner before leaving

Guernsey, my services would have gone unrecorded. When a person or an organisation has to be nudged into expressing thanks, then the thanks have little true value. I was reminded of the Garrick Theatre, Southport, in 1934, when Professor Cherio had, as a favour to a mutual friend, cast my horoscope. At the time Cherio was world-famous, an acknowledged leader in his field of horoscope. I had never concerned myself previously with his forecasts, but now reminded of it, rediscovered his predictions. It was in his own handwriting, and quite lengthy.

"Yours will be a hard struggle for survival. No element of luck or chance sways your life. You will receive no recognition in a public sense for anything which you may do in your public life. Self satisfaction is the most you can ever hope for or achieve".

In April of the following year I retired from the secretaryship of the Formby and Crosby Chambers which in the meantime I had amalgamated under the title Mid-Sefton Chamber. My final act was to organise a dinner to coincide with the A.G.M., and I was fortunate in that the then member of Parliament for Crosby was Mrs. Shirley Williams, and she readily accepted my invitation to attend as our guest speaker.

It was an enjoyable evening and Shirley Williams and I, as table companions, chatted agreeably together, naturally about politics. She is quite charming, and my kind of speaker. A rolling style off the cuff, and undoubtedly sincere.

There is an outstanding incident which cannot go without being recorded. I refer to the death of my dear friend George Porrit, God Rest His Soul. I have had very few real friends in my life, and of them all, his friendship was one which survived many years. The others were of short duration — Billy Cadwell in my pre-Blackshirt days in Southport; Jim Bellini and Vic King during my Blackshirt days in Hull, Dorothy Barton and Bernard Tennant, and until his death, Stanley Hull.

George fitted into a different category because we came from a similar background in Blackburn, though we did not meet until the late 1940s. We both knew that for a number of years he had been living on borrowed time though we never spoke of it. Yet it still came as a shock to me when the end came. I never realised just how much I would miss him.

Chapter Five

Mosley Man

July 1983 saw the screening of the BBC2 documentary: 'Britain in the Thirties', one episode of which dealt with Oswald Mosley and his North Country Blackshirts. Together with the late Dick Bellamy, Bob Row, Phil Sutherst, and Bill Wood we were able to present what in my opinion was the most unbiased portrayal of Mosley and his Movement that television has ever screened.

I was more than satisfied with my contribution and was delighted to later receive Lady Mosley's accolade of thanks. I wonder if I shall ever have another opportunity of publicly declaring my political faith? Probably not. I did at least exploit what chances came my way. As I said at the conclusion of that programme, I am proud to have nailed my colours to his mast. I have been asked many times over the years why I joined Oswald Mosley, and the reasons, though varied, remain the same.

I had originally been impressed by his early newsreel screenings during his Labour Party days, and his resignation speech from MacDonald's Government influenced me greatly. He carried an outward conviction of honesty and integrity. He appeared to know the problems of the times so thoroughly, and expressed his solutions so succinctly and with such conviction, that my inquiring mind was eased, and my disturbed spirit was soothed.

This was perhaps not clear to me at the time, but what I did know was that here was a man I could follow, no matter what the risk, no matter what the danger, no matter what the cost. The more I heard him speak, the more I felt bathed in that aura of light which always seemed to surround him, the more committed I became. My loyalty to him has never wavered.

I have also often been asked if the wearing of the black shirt helped to eradicate class barriers, and the simple answer to that is that within British Union I was never conscious of class barriers.

In those pre-war days the wearing of a monocle often signified snobbery. I only knew of one monocled Blackshirt. His name was Ned Warburton. I met him on numerous occasions and it never appeared strange or unusual to see him marching, or fighting, side by side with a London docker, Norfolk farmer or Lancashire textile worker. We were all Mosley's Blackshirts, members of an elite, a true band of brothers united by a bond of friendship that would last all our lives.

Ned, son of a Lancashire village blacksmith, had joined Mosley in the New Party and at 21, was hit in the eye by a communist hurled brick, blinding him for life, during the 'battle of Stockton-on-Tees' in 1933, one of the BUF's greatest street battles.

For weeks before the day, our small handful of members at Stockton had been molested by a Red mob and their meetings broken up. It came to a head when our principal northern speaker, Captain Vincent Collier, holding a meeting single-handed, was attacked and threatened with lynching.

A week later, a picked 100-strong contingent of Blackshirts from Manchester, Teeside and Tyneside, paraded in Middlesbrough and marched to Stockton's Market Square where our local lads were struggling to hold a meeting, faced by a hostile crowd estimated by the 12-strong police force present at 10,000, the majority of whom were Communists imported into the town for the occasion.

Ultimately, as our speakers endeavoured to make themselves heard, and to stop the fusillade of bricks and potatoes with inserted razor blades, the Blackshirts moved forward like a machine and in fierce fighting drove the Red section of the crowd 40 yards back across the square. After returning to the platform, they again made determined sweeps against the reassembling Reds, and after hours of such actions fought their way to the railway station where the last battle was successfully fought before entraining.

It was in one of these sweeps that Ned Warburton was felled, was cut off and carried struggling by a group of Reds who were going to 'chuck him in the river'. Fortunately, a group of uncommitted locals outside a pub saw the incident, attacked the Reds and rescued him, bandaged his head and got him back to the Blackshirts during a lull in the fighting.

Ned remained an active Blackshirt and shortly after was to write in "Blackshirt" — "There are things happening in England today that stink in the nostrils of all honest men. Behind all the superficial clowning and pageant of buffoonery and burlesque (the politicians), is misery and hunger in Clydeside and Tyneside. In Lancashire and South Wales women and children know hunger and despair. If I had been content with the role of spectator I should have been guilty of cowardice and betrayal".

A few years later, in 1937, Ned and his brother Johnny rescued Unity Mitford, Lady Mosley's sister, from a hostile crowd in Hyde Park, a story that went around the world. During the war he served in the Pioneer Corps, and in its final days was selected to organise German Army units who had surrendered intact in Denmark and North Germany, for possible use against an advancing Red Army into Western Europe.

Quite recently I was asked if I was still convinced that Mosley and his Movement were right. This requires careful answering so as not to convey wrong impressions. Mosley's approach to, his analysis of, and his basic answers to the economic questions of the days before the war and since the war, were invariably correct.

He did, however, in my opinion, make some psychological errors in the propaganda field. I think it was a mistake in 1936 to adopt, as he later admitted, a military style uniform of breeches and knee boots. If we had restricted ourselves to the black shirt of the fencing jacket style, the charge of militarism may never have been levelled against us. Also if we had used the title of 'British Union Party' antagonism may not have been as intense.

Am I still proud of my association with Oswald Mosley and his Movement? To this I reply that the days when I marched through the towns and cities of this land in the company of Mosley and his Blackshirts were the proudest of my life. His politics attracted many bitterly disillusioned ex-service men and women, and thousands more disenchanted young men and women. Mosley was in a hurry. Why? Because he wanted to rebuild Britain, and above all avoid another war.

He failed because he ran out of time, and because he was deliberately denied press and radio. This 'Great Smother' operated from 1934 on. His opponents knew only too well that when the people heard Mosley, the people began to think, and in the main found themselves in agreement with his analysis and solutions. Former Labour Cabinet Minister, R.H.S. Crossman wrote:

"Mosley was spurned by Whitehall, Fleet Street, and every party leader at Westminster, simply and solely because he was right[4].

Hannen Swaffer, a leading Socialist journalist of his day, wrote in 1943 under the headline 'SAVED BY THE WAR' that it was

"left to the war and 18b to deal effectively with Mosley and his movement. . . Yes, but for the war we might today have been a Fascist country"[5].

My seven pre-war years in British Union were years of excitement, almost of adventure, with a commitment of near-religious fervour to a man and an ideal that gave me an unforgettable experience of comradeship that perhaps no man can expect to meet with again.

---

4   New Statesman 27th October 1961
5   World's Press News 5th Oct 1943

The death of Oswald Mosley on 3rd December 1980 created a void in my life which nothing can replace. I suffered a permanent devastation of spirit which simply defies description, and which cannot be assuaged. No words can ever convey or express my sense of loss. Mosley was unique. For me and many others, he was the greatest Englishman of his age. His repudiation by the Establishment was, and remains, England's tragedy. I miss him more than I can say.

Now nearing the end of my life, I sometimes ask myself what was it for? How could so much effort, so much involvement, dedication and belief, how could it all come to nothing?

Surely there is something left upon which a New Ideal can be built? I hope so. It is eternal hope. I was never truly a politician. I was — and remain — a Mosley man. One hears today much talk about "Thatcherism", though nobody knows what it is. In the thirties no one ever referred to Mosleyism, but if I believed in anything it was Mosleyism. I believed in the man. I believed in his honesty, his sincerity, his integrity, his ability, his vision, and because I believed in these things, and because I found all the other politicians wanting in comparison, I was convinced that my dedication was true, and not wasted. And so I hope that the great crusade which inspired tens of thousands of our British people will have lit a torch whose flame will inspire anew. For it is certain that our country has need of it.

Someone once asked me to compare Oswald Mosley with any previous figure in English history, and the nearest I could come up with was a combination of two, both boyhood heroes; Hereward the Wake and Simon de Montfort. Mosley represented the past and had this great vision of the future, and he married the two in a new ideology. I was and remain a Mosley man. For me "His Spirit Lives".

John Charnley died on 27 December 1988 shortly after completing this story. His last words to a younger, old comrade just before Christmas when he knew his days were numbered were:

"Do not mourn for me, Johnny, I have had a good life, a wonderful wife, walked in the shadow of the greatest Englishman that ever lived, and have shared the comradeship of some of the finest men in human history. Carry on the ever upward struggle in Mosley's image. I shall be ever with you".—

* 9 7 8 1 9 0 8 4 7 6 4 3 2 *